# MIRACLES
## ARE HEAVEN SENT

HONOR
BOOKS

Tulsa, Oklahoma

# Introduction

**MIRACLES!**
We delight in them.
They intrigue us.
We find them mysterious, awe-inspiring, spine-tingling, and on occasion, deeply thought-provoking.
We desire to experience them.
But truly . . . what are miracles?

Is every serendipitous coincidence a miracle? Is every good deed, nice moment, or turn-around point in life a miracle? Is every process of nature ultimately a miracle — both the processes we know and those we have not yet discovered? Perhaps. Ultimately, miracles are what you define them to be.

In *Miracles Are Heaven Sent*, however, we used a three-fold criterion for selecting these stories and statements about miracles.

*First, miracles are regarded as "works of God."*
They are divine in origin and initiated according
to the will of God. Indeed, they are HEAVEN SENT.
As such, they are manifestations of God's creativity.
They bear the marks of His presence and power at
work in human affairs and the natural order.

*Second, miracles are inextricably related to life.*
In some cases, they cause or promote life.
In some cases, they extend life. In still other
cases, they bring about a peaceful end to one's
current life, and pave the way toward a new
and more wonderful afterlife. It is perhaps

because miracles are connected to the awesome and mysterious force of life that we find them so compelling and so desirable.

*Third, genuine miracles point us toward God's love.* They become examples to us of a benevolent and loving God at work in our lives and in the lives of others. We are attracted to God our Heavenly Father— and to His Son Jesus Christ, and to His Holy Spirit— through miracles. They in some way woo us to a greater awareness of His presence, and they create in us a greater desire to know Him intimately.

The selections chosen for this book speak with a number of different voices. Some of the entries are excerpts from books, plays, and sermons, including a few direct quotes and paraphrases from the Bible. Some of the selections are prayers, songs, or poems. While some teach and some inspire, others simply tell a story. Some are expressions of opinion. None of the entries, however, are fiction. All address real issues, real people and real circumstances.

Miracles inspire us to "believe." They create in us hope that maybe, just maybe, we might experience a genuine life-altering miracle for ourselves. Toward that end, we invite you to use these entries as "food for your faith" so that you might begin with new zeal to . . .

**Expect a miracle in your own life!**

The Christian faith is a faith in the miraculous; if we do not believe in miracles, we do not believe in Him.

Did the palsied man arise? Was the man with the withered hand made whole? Was the lady with the flow of blood healed by touching His garment? Did Lazarus actually come forth from the tomb?

We must believe or not believe, accept or not accept; there is no room for any middle ground of half belief or half doubt.

— **Will Oursler**
*The Road to Faith*
1960

Miracles, like anything else, can be counterfeited. And, as with good counterfeit money, the authentic is sometimes difficult to separate from the phony. In some cases only close examination of all the essential features by a trained observer will distinguish the difference. However, in most cases the earmarks of a miracle are very clear.

## A. MIRACLES DIFFER FROM ANOMALIES

The only similarity between a miracle and an anomaly is the unusual character of both—being odd, they both arouse interest. Beyond this there is no real similarity. Hence, simply because an event is unusual—no matter how unusual—the believer has no right to claim it is miraculous. Unless there are some theological, moral, and doctrinal purposes evident, one has no right to claim an event is a miracle. That is, there must be a theistic context for a miracle, for without signs of intelligent intervention no unusual event can be claimed to be a miracle. Odd things happen and without these divine "earmarks" they are simply that—odd. Without the other divine characteristics, the anomaly is presumed to be a natural

event with a knowable cause. As scientific research proceeds, perhaps the cause will be found. On the other hand, unless the anomaly can be repeated, predicted, or brought under some natural control, there is no reason to revise any scientific law. It is simply an exception with no known natural explanation. In this sense, anomalies and miracles are alike. They differ in that a miracle in its theistic context gives evidence of intelligent (divine) intervention to produce the unusual event.

## B. MIRACLES DIFFER FROM MAGIC

Here we speak not of black magic or occult activity, but simply of illusions, sleight-of-hand, or trickery. The only thing magic has in common with miracles is that both are unusual. To be sure, magic is a kind of "wonder" (Exodus 7-8). It is amazing to those who do not know the trick. But it has none of the other characteristics of a miracle. In fact, unlike an anomaly, there are known explanations for the magical wonders—known to magicians. Unlike miracles, magic as such is amoral. It does not bring glory to God (it really brings honor to the magician), and there are usually no divine truth claims connected with it. If there were supernatural claims connected with magical tricks, they could be exposed by another person who knows the tricks or by scientific tests for the hidden wires, mirrors, etc., that create the illusion.

## C. MIRACLES DIFFER FROM DEMONIC ACTIVITY

The same biblical words used of divine miracles are used of demonic acts. Jesus warned, "False Christs and false prophets will arise and will show great signs and wonders, so as to mislead, if possible, even the elect" (Matthew 24:24 NASB). Paul warns of the Antichrist "whose coming is in accord with the activity of Satan, with all power and signs and false wonders, and with all the deception of wickedness" (2 Thessalonians 2:9,10 NASB). John speaks of the "beast" to come who "performs great signs, so that he even makes fire come down out of heaven to the earth in the presence of men" (Revelation 13:13 NASB). Later, John speaks of the "spirits of demons, performing signs" (Revelation 16:14 NASB) and of the "false prophet who performed the signs . . . by which he deceived those who had received the mark of the beast and those who worshipped his image" (Revelation 19:20 NASB).

While some believers in biblical miracles have questioned whether these satanic signs should be called "miracles," there seems to be no reason to deny that they are supernatural. If a miracle by definition is an act of God

that brings glory to God and good to the world, etc., then of course a demonic act is not a miracle. On the other hand, it seems evident that if one is going to believe in acts of God on the basis of the biblical record, then on this same basis he ought to believe that there are evil spirit beings who can perform highly unusual acts that the Bible calls "signs" and "wonders."

If, then, the Bible claims there are at least two supernatural sources for unusual "signs" in the world, how does one tell them apart? The answer involves several "tests" (1 John 4:1) that the believer is urged to apply, all of which amount to saying that satanic "signs" have satanic (evil) characteristics and divine miracles have Godlike (good) characteristics. Numerous evils are mentioned in the Bible, such as idolatry (1 Corinthians 10:19), immorality (Ephesians 2:2), divination (Deuteronomy 18:10), false prophecies (Deuteronomy 18:22), occult activity (Deuteronomy 18:14), worshipping other gods (Deuteronomy 13:1,2), deceptive activity (2 Thessalonians 2:9), contacting the dead (Deuteronomy 18:11,12), messages contrary to those revealed through true prophets (Galatians 1:8), and prophecies that do not center on Jesus Christ (Revelation 19:10). And, as with any other counterfeit and deception, one must know the characteristics of good and of evil and then look carefully to see which are connected with the unusual event.

Whenever there was any serious question in the Bible as to which events were of God, a contest followed in which good triumphed over evil by an even greater miracle than the magic or satanic signs. In the contest between Moses and the Egyptian magicians, they could not reduplicate the sign of turning dust into life and gave up, crying, "This is the finger of God" (Exodus 8:18,19). In the dispute between Moses and Korah the earth opened up and swallowed Korah and company and the dispute ended abruptly (Numbers 16). Likewise, Elijah triumphed over the false prophets of Baal on Mount Carmel when fire came from heaven and consumed the water-soaked sacrifices (1 Kings 18). In the New Testament, Jesus and the apostles triumphed over evil spirits and even exorcised them (Acts 16). When necessary, the supreme God proves Himself supreme.

## Summary

Before a miracle can be known to have occurred, it must be defined. We must know what we are looking for before

we can know that we have found it. First, miracles stand in contrast to "nature," which is God's regular and predictable way of working in the world. Miracles are an unusual and  unpredictable way in which God sometimes intervenes in the events of the world.

A survey of the Bible shows that a miracle is an effect that may look no different from any other unusual effect, but the characteristic feature is that it has a supernatural cause. It is performed with divine power, according to the divine mind, for a divine purpose, in order to authenticate a divine message or, perhaps, just to demonstrate God's compassion.

The biblical description of miracles uses three mains words: power, wonder, and sign. Respectively, these words designate the source (in God), the nature (unusual), and the purpose of a miracle.

The miraculous event would be looked on as unusual because it does not fit some regular pattern of nature. From the scientific, observational viewpoint, it might appear to be simply an anomaly of nature; i.e., a natural event that has not yet been shown to fit a lawful pattern. But, in the case of a miracle, there would be a context of theistic claims to give it intelligibility. Without that context, which characterized Bible miracles, the alleged miracle could never have been known. It would have remained forever an "anomaly" of nature.

Spelled out in theological terms, a miracle usually manifests five characteristics: the unusual, the theological, the moral, the doctrinal, and the teleological. Miracles can be distinguished from anomalies and magic, since the latter two share only one of these characteristics—the unusual.

While satanic signs are not amoral, they do differ from miracles in their discernibly evil characteristics. In short, biblical miracles are acts of God to confirm the Word of God through a prophet of God to the people of God.

Finally, we can conclude that miracles are possible only within a theistic universe. If God exists, then miracles are possible. Further, if God exists, then miracles are identifiable in terms of some Godlike characteristics (theological, moral, etc.).

— **Norman L. Geisler**

*Miracles and Modern Thought* by Norman L. Geisler, copyright © 1982, Probe Ministries, Richardson, TX 75081. Used by permission.

$J$esus taught:

"Just believe it — that I am in the Father and the Father is in me. Or else believe it because of the mighty miracles you have seen me do.

"In solemn truth I tell you, anyone believing in me shall do the same miracles I have done, and even greater ones, because I am going to be with the Father. You can ask him for anything, using my name, and I will do it, for this will bring praise to the Father because of what I, the Son, will do for you. Yes, ask anything, using my name, and I will do it!"

**— John 14:11-14 (TLB)**
*HOLY BIBLE*

# LOVE

where there had been no love.

## LIFE

where there had seemed to be no life.

## HOPE

where there was no reason to hope.

## FAITH

in spite of all appearances.

In these lie miracles.

— **Anonymous**

A child found alive and well after 72 hours of being trapped under a ton of rubble . . .

The first birthday of twins born so prematurely that neither was expected to live . . .

An infant rushed to its mother's arms from the ruins of a bomb-blasted building . . .

A young boy who overcomes leukemia to laugh and play again with his friends . . .

A little girl pulled safely from the deep shaft of an abandoned well . . .

A baby carried safely from the fiery crash of an airplane . . .

A toddler who emerges unscathed after two days and nights of wandering alone in the woods . . .

Is any miracle greater than that which gives life's opportunity to a child?

The greatest miracle in the world is that God loves us and His Son died for us. His love for us is, and forever will remain, an inexplicable mystery. The most amazing supernatural event ever to occur was the incarnation and then the death of the eternal Son in the place of sinful humanity, followed by His bodily resurrection. Surely the greatest wonder is that by faith alone in Jesus Christ we receive the gift of eternal life. Surely the greatest power any human will ever know is the power of the cross of Jesus Christ. Through the cross we not only have forgiveness but also access into God's glorious presence.

The power of Christ's death is so great that no Christian has to live under any moral bondage. No Christian has to be at the mercy of lust, anger, sin, fear, death, or Satan. Surely this good news is the greatest news that has ever been given. Surely this message is greater than any miracles accompanying it. Surely the gospel is capable of capturing the hearts of people without requiring any accompanying miracles!

**— Jack Deere**

Speaking about Mary, the mother of Jesus . . .

Mary's humanness is essential to our fully appreciating her miracle. Only then can we see how determined God was to become incarnate as one of us, and to work a wonder to achieve it. But to see that wonder is also to see how committed He is to work beyond our helplessness; to move in upon us with His ability to redeem our hopelessness as well. In Mary, the same One Who spoke into the chaotic disorder of the Genesis "void" and brought light and life, spoke promise into the tainted humanness of her virgin womb and begot the Light of the world—bringing Life to all humankind.

Since that moment, the Light has kept increasing, and His Life has kept on multiplying in thousands of "wombs of circumstance" where other members of Adam's race open themselves—first to Mary's Son, and then to the patterns of possibility revealed in her miracle.

The Mary miracle first happened to an ordinary sinner in an ordinary town to set forth this lesson for all learners: Nothing is impossible where you live either—no matter who you are. Because salvation has come to save, this greatest of all miracles—once received—holds in it the seeds of any number of wonders.

— **Jack Hayford**

A miracle properly so called is when something is done outside the order of nature. But it is not enough for a miracle if something is done outside the order of any particular nature; for otherwise anyone would perform a miracle by throwing a stone upwards, as such a thing is outside the order of the stone's nature. So for something to be called a miracle it is required that it be against the order of the whole created nature. But God alone can do this, because, whatever an angel or any other creature does by its own power, is according to the order of created nature, and thus it is not a miracle. Hence, God alone can work miracles.

— **St. Thomas Aquinas**
*Summa Theologica, Part I*
Question 110, Article 4

# MIRACLES
## ARE HEAVEN SENT

Belief in the miraculous is integral to Christianity. Theologians who discard all miracles, thus obliging themselves to deny Jesus' incarnation and resurrection, the two supreme miracles of Scripture, should not claim to be Christians: the claim is not valid. The rejection of miracles by yesterday's scientists sprang not from science but from the dogma of a universe of absolute uniformity that scientists brought to their scientific work. There is nothing irrational about believing that God Who made the world can still intrude creatively into it. Christians should recognize that it is not faith in the biblical miracles, and in God's ability to work miracles today should he so wish, but doubt about these things, that is unreasonable.

— **J. I. Packer**

From: Concise Theology, A Guide to Historic Christian Beliefs By: J. I. Packer, copyright © 1993 Foundation for Reformation. Used by permission of Tyndale House Publishers, Inc. All rights reserved.

The Christian life is stamped all through with impossibility. Human nature cannot come anywhere near what Jesus Christ demands, and any rational being facing His demands honestly, says, "It can't be done, apart from a miracle." Exactly.

— Oswald Chambers

In all the world we see the miracles of God.

Tiny seeds you can hold in your hand become huge trees that can be made into wood to build houses.

Birds that sing and soar in brilliant blue sky;
Springtime and harvest: Babies and families.

The miracles of God's creation can fill us with life and joy because of God's greatest miracle . . . Jesus.

He became like us so that we can become like Him.

How does the tiny seed become a mighty tree?
It's a miracle.

How does the sparrow fly in the boundless sky?
It's a miracle.

How can peace come to the spirit that has only known life's storms?

How can a world that someone's made so cold change and become warm?

It's the miracle of Jesus,
The greatest miracle of all.
He's so far beyond our simple minds,
Yet so near when sinners call.
All it takes is honest praying
From an open, seeking heart,
And the miracle of Jesus can start.

The baby Jesus cried, and mother Mary sighed.
"It's a miracle!"
It was the Master's plan, He'd live as God and man.
It's a miracle.
And the tomb just could not hold Him, the stone was
rolled away;
Our Savior rose up to the sky, He'll return for us one
day.
It's the miracle of Jesus,
The greatest miracle of all.
He's so far beyond our simple minds,
Yet so near when sinners call.
All it takes is honest praying
From an open, seeking heart,
And the miracle of Jesus can start.

**— Phill McHugh and Corliss Nelson**
River Oaks Music, Nashville, TN, 1989

The fitness of the Christian miracles and their difference from these mythological miracles, lies in the fact that they show invasion by a Power which is not alien. They are what might be expected to happen when she is invaded not simply by a god, but by the God of Nature: by a Power which is outside her jurisdiction not as a foreigner but as a sovereign. They proclaim that He Who has come is not merely a king, but the King, her King and ours.

— **C. S. Lewis**
*Miracles*

Jesus gave a radically new meaning to the "language" of the miracles: they are signs of the kingdom, signs of what God wants to do and is already doing for humankind in Jesus. . .

If this interrelationship between the miracles of Jesus and His message of the kingdom of God is disregarded, neither the miracles nor the message of the kingdom will be understood correctly. The connection between healings and the kingdom of God is particularly clear: "Heal the sick there, and say to them, 'The kingdom of God has come near to you'" (Luke 10:9 NKJV).

**— Herman Hendricks**
*The Miracle Stories of the Synoptic Gospels*
1987

# MIRACLES
## ARE HEAVEN SENT

In the concentration camp where I was imprisoned many years ago, sometimes bitterness and hatred tried to enter my heart when people were so cruel to my sister and me. Then I learned this prayer, a "thank you" for Romans 5:5.

"Thank You, Lord Jesus, that You have brought into my heart the love of God through the Holy Spirit, Who is given to me. Thank You, Father, that Your love in me is victorious over the bitterness in me and the cruelty around me."

After I prayed it, I experienced the miracle that there was no room for bitterness in my heart anymore.

**— Corrie ten Boom**
*Clippings from My Notebook*

The greatest miracle that God can do today is to take an unholy man out of an unholy world, and make that man holy and put him back into that unholy world and keep him holy in it.

— Leonard Ravenhill

• • • **I**f we turn our eyes to invisible things, then certain it is that it is a greater miracle, by preaching of the Word and virtue of prayer, to convert a sinner than to raise up a dead man.

— **From Dialogues of St. Gregory the Great**

The new birth is a miracle of life. It is something we accept as real, but not comprehensible. Life is not so fully understood that we can pour it into tiny molds of our limited reason.

— **Billy Graham**
The Quotable Billy Graham
Compiled and Edited by
Cort R. Flint and the Staff of
Quote Anderson, SC:
Droke House, 1966

Saul was still breathing threats to slaughter the Lord's disciples. He went to the high priest and asked for letters addressed to the synagogues in Damascus, that would authorize him to arrest and take to Jerusalem any followers of the Way, men or women, that he might find.

It happened that while he was travelling to Damascus and approaching the city, suddenly a light from heaven shone all round him. He fell to the ground, and then he heard a voice saying, "Saul, Saul, why are you persecuting me?" "Who are you, Lord?" he asked, and the answer came, "I am Jesus, whom you are persecuting. Get up and go into the city, and you will be told what you are to do." The men traveling with Saul stood there speechless, for though they heard the voice they could see no one. Saul got up from the ground, but when he opened his eyes he could see nothing at all, and they had to lead him into Damascus by the hand. For three days he was without his sight and took neither food nor drink.

There was a disciple in Damascus called Ananias and he had a vision in which the Lord said to him, "Ananias!" When he replied, "Here I am, Lord," the Lord said, "Get up and go to Straight Street and ask at the house of Judas for someone called Saul, who comes from Tarsus. At this moment he is praying, and has seen a man called Ananias coming in and laying hands on him to give him back his sight."

But in response, Ananias said, "Lord, I have heard from many people about this man and all the harm he has been doing to your holy people in Jerusalem. He has come here with a warrant from the chief priests to arrest everybody who invokes your name." The Lord replied, "Go, for this man is my chosen instrument to bring my name before gentiles and kings and before the people of Israel; I myself will show him how much he must suffer for my name." Then Ananias went. He entered the house, and laid his hands on Saul and said, "Brother Saul, I have been sent by the Lord Jesus, who appeared to you on your way here, so that you may recover your sight and be filled with the Holy Spirit." It was as though scales fell away from his eyes and immediately he was able to see again. So he got up and was baptized, and after taking some food he regained his strength.

**— Acts 9:1-19 (The New Jerusalem Bible)**
*HOLY BIBLE*

$T$o the true disciple a miracle only manifests the power and love which are silently at work everywhere as divinely in the gift of daily bread as in the miraculous multiplication of the loaves.

**— Frederick William Robertson**
*Encyclopedia of Religious Quotations*

Virtually all the miracles attributed to Jesus are directly associated with some lesson He was trying to teach or some insight He wanted to give to His disciples. The real question to be asked about any miracle is not how it happened but why: what was God saying to us in this significant act?

— **Louis Cassels**

s [Jesus] passed by, He saw a man blind from birth. And His disciples asked Him, saying, "Rabbi, who sinned, this man or his parents, that he should be born blind?"

Jesus answered, "It was neither that this man sinned, nor his parents; but it was in order that the works of God might be displayed in him.

"We must work the works of Him who sent Me, as long as it is day; night is coming, when no man can work.

"While I am in the world, I am the light of the world."

When He had said this, He spat on the ground, and made clay of the spittle, and applied the clay to his eyes, and said to him, "Go, wash in the pool of Siloam" (which is translated, Sent).  And so he went away and washed, and came back seeing.

**— John 9:1-7 (NASB)**
*HOLY BIBLE*

When Jesus had crossed over again in the boat to the other side, a great multitude gathered about Him; and He stayed by the seashore.

And one of the synagogue officials named Jairus came up, and upon seeing Him, fell at His feet, and entreated Him earnestly, saying, "My little daughter is at the point of death; please come and lay Your hands on her, that she may get well and live."

And He went off with him; and a great multitude was following Him and pressing in on Him.

And a woman who had had a hemorrhage for twelve years, and had endured much at the hands of many physicians, and had spent all that she had and was not helped at all, but rather had grown worse, after hearing about Jesus, came up in the crowd behind Him, and touched His cloak.

For she thought, "If I just touch His garments, I shall get well."

And immediately the flow of her blood was dried up; and she felt in her body that she was healed of her affliction.

And immediately Jesus, perceiving in Himself that the power proceeding from Him had gone forth, turned

around in the crowd and said, "Who touched My garments?"

And His disciples said to Him, "You see the multitude pressing in on You, and You say, 'Who touched Me?'"

And He looked around to see the woman who had done this.

But the woman fearing and trembling, aware of what had happened to her, came and fell down before Him, and told Him the whole truth.

And He said to her, "Daughter, your faith has made you well; go in peace, and be healed of your affliction."

While He was still speaking, they came from the house of the synagogue official, saying, "Your daughter has died; why trouble the Teacher any more?"

But Jesus, overhearing what was being spoken, said to the synagogue official, "Do not be afraid any longer, only believe."

And He allowed no one to follow with Him, except Peter and James and John the brother of James.

And they came to the house of the synagogue official; and He beheld a commotion, and people loudly weeping and wailing.

And entering in, He said to them, "Why make a commotion and weep? The child has not died, but is asleep."

And they were laughing at Him. But putting them all out, He took along the child's father and mother and His own companions, and entered the room where the child was.

And taking the child by the hand, He said to her, "Talitha kum!" (which translated means, "Little girl, I say to you, arise!")

And immediately the girl got up and began to walk; for she was twelve years old. And immediately they were completely astounded.

**— Mark 5:21-42 (NASB)**
*HOLY BIBLE*

$T$he miracles of Jesus were the ordinary works of His Father, wrought small and swift that we might take them in.

— George MacDonald
Unspoken Sermons,
Second Series
The Cause of Spiritual
Stupidity
George MacDonald,
365 Readings, New York:
Macmillan Publishing Co.
*1947*

A seventeen-year-old New York girl, Alisha, was dying with tuberculosis. Her physician, who was a Christian, told her, "You are going to die and there is nothing we can do. Tuberculosis has set in. One lung is gone and the other is half gone. I am going to send you home so that you can spend your remaining days with your family."

At home, she lay in her bed desperately ill and in an oxygen tent. Her body dwindled down to less than seventy pounds. Propped up so that she could read her Bible, Alisha began to prepare herself for her death. She read from 1 Peter 2:24: "Who his own self bare our sins in his own body on the tree, that we, being dead to sins, should live unto righteousness . . . ." When she read these words, she put her Bible down and began to praise God.

Weeping, she said, "Oh, Lord, I will be so glad to see You. I know I am going to die. Doctors can't do any more for me. But thank You for saving me. Thank You for washing me in the blood." Then she went back to reading the verse.

". . . being dead to sins, should live unto righteousness; by whose stripes ye were healed." The words lit up like a neon sign on the page.

"Lord," she prayed again, "I just finished praising You for the first part of the verse, now I am going to praise You for the second part. You have already healed me. Jesus, I am sorry I won't be seeing You right now. I plan on staying around here awhile!"

Then she started praising God for perfect health. Next she unzipped the oxygen tent. "Mama, come here quick!" Expecting that her daughter was dying, her mother rushed in. "What is it, baby?" Excitedly, Alisha showed her mother the verse promising her healing. But instead of joy, her mother began crying.

"The doctor told us that you would begin to lose your mind when death was near."

"But," Alisha insisted, "I'm not going to die. In fact, I'm hungry. Go make me some eggs, bacon, biscuits, and orange juice!" This alarmed Alisha's mother even more since she knew her daughter had eaten practically nothing for nearly ten months. Thinking the girl was delirious, she tucked her back in bed, zipped up the oxygen tent, and sneaked out of the room.

No sooner had the door closed than Alisha unzipped the tent, turned back the covers, and put her unsteady feet on the floor. She went to the closet and pulled out one of her prettiest dresses and put it on. Because of her weight loss, it hung on her like a bathrobe. She put on her slippers and started downstairs. In the kitchen, her astonished mother was putting the finishing touches on the breakfast meal.

Alisha sat down to eat and prayed, "Lord, bless this food to my brand-new body. I am not going to die! I am going to live!"

Strengthened by a few good meals, Alisha went to the doctor the next day. He was more than astonished to see her standing in his office. But his astonishment became awe when he examined the x-rays to find that Alisha apparently had two brand-new lungs, with no trace of tuberculosis.

*Eyewitness to the Miraculous* by R.W. Shambach,
copyright © 1993, Harrison House Publishers, Tulsa, OK.

# MIRACLES
## ARE HEAVEN SENT

Christians see answers to prayer every day, and we should not water down our definition of miracle so much that every answer to prayer is called a miracle. But when an answer to prayer is so remarkable that people involved in it are amazed and acknowledge God's power at work in an unusual way, then it seems appropriate to call it a miracle. This is consistent with our definition,* and seems supported by the Biblical evidence that works of God that aroused people's awe and wonder were called miracles (Greek dunamis).

But whether we adopt a broad or narrow definition of miracle, all should agree that if God really does work in answer to our prayers, whether in common or uncommon ways, it is important that we recognize this and give thanks to Him. As well, we should not ignore the answered prayer or go to great lengths to devise possible "natural causes" to explain away what God has in fact done. Although we must be careful not to exaggerate in reporting details of answers to prayer, we must also avoid the opposite error of failing to glorify and thank God for what He has done.

*A miracle is a less common kind of God's activity in which He arouses people's awe and wonder and bears witness to Himself.*
— **Wayne Grudem**

*E*vangelist R. W. Schambach tells of an unusual *healing that took place in conjunction with one of his revivals:* We were setting up a tent in Sacramento, California, and getting ready for the afternoon service. A woman brought her child, who had crossed eyes, for prayer. I saw the woman weeping in the back so I went to her and said, "What's wrong?"

"Oh," she said, "I brought my daughter who has had crossed eyes since birth. I came from San Francisco for a prayer card but you aren't having a service. I have traveled hundreds of miles. What am I going to do? I knew if I could just get her under the tent, her eyes would be healed."

I said, "Where is your daughter?"

The mother, sobbing, gestured to a little girl nearby. "Here she is." I got down on my knees and looked at the little girl's face—and saw two straight eyes.

I said, "Are you sure this is your daughter?"

"I ought to know my own daughter," she replied.

I said, "You told me she had crossed eyes."

The mother got down on her knees and looked at her daughter's eyes. No one laid hands on the girl. She didn't have to get a prayer card. She grabbed that girl and

started running around the tent. God had performed a miracle. When did God do it? God took her at her word. I heard her say, "I knew if I could just get my daughter under that tent. . . ." I believe the moment she stepped inside that tent, the crossed eyes became straight because God honored her faith.

*Eyewitness to the Miraculous* by R.W. Shambach, copyright © 1993, Harrison House Publishers, Tulsa, OK.

On November 14, 1983, two American students named David and Ray teamed up to pray for the 40,000 Tira people in Africa. The large group had no Bible in their native tongue.

Two and a half years later, other Christians, Jerry and Jan, joined them in praying daily for the Tira. Then, in March 1990, Jane and Marjeanne wrote to the Bibleless Peoples Prayer Project of Wycliffe Bible Translators, asking for the name of a Bibleless people to pray for. They too began praying that God would somehow move someone to translate His Word for the Tira people.

In August 1990, we heard that Avajani, a young Tira man, was beginning to translate the Bible. Great news! We wrote, telling him of those praying and how he was an answer to their prayers.

"I'm grateful," Avajani wrote back. "I have never known that there are teams praying for the Tira people. It is wonderful news to me. The same year and month when David and Ray started praying, I got saved. I was accepted for theological studies. . . and now I have finished. Jane and Marjeanne can praise the Lord with me, too! In March 1990, a miracle happened. I met a man (a Wycliffe translator) who was able to arrange for me to study Biblical translation principles and linguistics.

"God did another miracle. Many young Tira have become Christians. Many Tira from different denominations like the translation." Today, seven years after David and Ray began praying in faith—with no idea of how God was answering — the Bible is being translated for 40,000 new readers.

Early in his career, the great Chinese writer and preacher Watchman Nee spent a New Year's holiday with five other young believers trying to evangelize the village of Mei-hwa. The men had difficulty getting a hearing amid all the noisy celebrations. By the ninth day the farmers and fishermen still weren't listening. One of the frustrated evangelists asked, "What's wrong? Why won't you believe?"

He was informed that Mei-hwa already had a reliable deity, Ta-Wang. The day of his festival, made known by divination, was fixed for January 11. For the past 286 years, the villagers affirmed, Ta-Wang had provided unfailing sunshine for the day he chose.

The headstrong evangelist exclaimed, "Then I promise you that our God—who is the true God—will make it rain on the eleventh." His hearers seized the challenge. If Jesus could make it rain on the eleventh they would certainly listen to him.

Watchman and the others with him were at first horrified by their brother's assertion. Was their God being presumptuously put on the spot? But after the men prayed very earnestly over the matter a phrase from Scripture flashed into Watchman's mind: "Where is the

God of Elijah?" Watchman felt assured that rain would fall on the eleventh. So the evangelists spread the challenge widely.

That evening their host informed that half of the village natives were fishermen who spent months out at sea and could be relied on to forecast the weather accurately for days ahead. The odds for rain on the eleventh seemed bad indeed. But again Watchman was assured by the words, "Where is the God of Elijah?"

On the morning of the eleventh the evangelists were awakened by brilliant sunlight shining through their window. Quietly they gathered for breakfast. No sign of a cloud in the sky. As they bowed to say grace, Watchman observed, "I think the time is up. Rain must come now. We can bring it to the Lord's remembrance." They did so.

The first drops of rain hit the roof tiles before their "Amen." As the men ate their rice, the drizzle became a steady shower. On being served a second bowl, Watchman paused to give thanks and ask for even heavier rain. It began coming down by the bucketfuls. At the end of breakfast the street outside was deep in water.

A few faithful Ta-Wang supporters had carried their idol in a sedan chair outside, hoping his presence would stop the shower. But once it was in the street the downpour came. After a few yards the bearers stumbled in the flood. Ta-Wang fell and fractured his jaw and left arm.

Still they would not acknowledge defeat. The faithful repaired Ta-Wang and made fresh divination. A mistake had been made. The festival was supposed to be on the fourteenth.

Watchman and his men retired to pray. They asked for three sunny days and rain at 6 P.M. on the fourteenth, when Ta-Wang's procession would begin.

For the next few days the evangelists preached to large audiences under blue skies. The fourteenth began as another perfect day. When evening approached, Watchman and his friends brought their request to God and, not a minute late, His answer came with torrential rains and floods.

Taken from *Against The Tide,* copyright © 1973, Angus I. Kinnear. Used by permission of Kingsway Publications, Lottbridge Drove, Eastbourne, BN23 6NT

Willliam had never been sick a day in his life. He had money in the bank and felt his future as a government employee was secure. Then suddenly he was stricken with severe spinal meningitis.

Paralyzed from head to toe, he spent more than three months in the hospital and grew only sicker and sicker. Specialists from all over the world were consulted on his case. His bank account dwindled and he had to sell his home in order to pay the overwhelming medical bills.

Then rheumatoid arthritis crept into every joint, causing unbearable pain. Finally he lapsed into a coma.

As William was Roman Catholic, a priest was called in to administer the last rites. Lying in the coma, William says that he was completely aware of what the priest was doing, but because of the paralysis, he was unable to respond in any way. The priest's actions confirmed for him that this was probably his last day on earth. Finally, the priest was finished; he took off his stole and went out the door. Suddenly another priest entered. But this one came through the *wall* instead of the door. There was something different about this priest. He was dressed all in white. He leaned down to the dying man and said, "William, you don't have any trouble. All you need is faith in God."

William couldn't respond except in his mind. *What kind of crazy priest is this?* he thought. I don't have any trouble? What do you call paralysis and this searing pain in my joints?

But the priest wasn't finished. "I am Jesus of Nazareth, and I am going to heal you right now. When I walk out of this room, I want you to get out of this bed. Shave, wash, and walk out of this hospital. Go to the first bookstore you can find and buy a Bible. Start reading from St. John's gospel. You will find the way to eternal life." Then the man turned around and walked back through the wall.

When the nurse came in, she found her comatose patient in the lavatory shaving. "Get back in that bed," she demanded. "You've already been administered the last rites; you're dying!"

"Cool it, honey," William grinned. "Another priest came in and administered the 'first rites' all over again and I'm going to *live.*

*Eyewitness to the Miraculous* by R.W. Shambach,
copyright © 1993, Harrison House Publishers, Tulsa, OK.

The choice that turns out to be best

Days of rain that yield to bright sunshine and blue skies the hour before the wedding

The rusty key that fits the lock

The phone call that provides vital information just moments before the decision must be made

Receiving a check in the mail on the day the bills are due

The fever that breaks at dawn

The unexpected visit from a long-lost friend on a day marked by loneliness

The missing wallet returned after days of frantic searching

An all-clear report when prevailing symptoms seemed to indicate trouble

Falling asleep, at last

Small miracles?
Or perhaps big?

It was a case of not being in the right place at the right time.

More than forty years ago, in a small church in the Midwest, there came a night like no other. It was so incredible, people still remember and talk about it.

Wednesday night was choir practice. Everyone knew that. Everyone knew that it started at 7:30 p.m. Every week. The twelve members of the choir were normally prompt, as were the pastor and his wife, the pianist, and the director.

But that incredible Wednesday night, something went wrong—or right.

What are the chances that *everyone* would arrive for practice at least five minutes late—especially when such a thing had never happened before? Astronomical. But that night, thank God, that's exactly what *did* happen.

Each person had some excuse for coming late—a car that wouldn't start, a homework assignment, a letter to write, a compelling radio program, a slow watch. Even so . . . *every* one of those people was running late.

"What's so significant about that?" you ask. "They still had time to practice their anthem, right?"

They might have . . . if a natural gas leak in the basement had not been enkindled by the furnace, causing an explosion that demolished the entire church...but none of the tardy singers . . . at precisely 7:30 p.m.

A doctor was driving up a mountain, headed to a resort area where he was scheduled to speak at a conference. Although he was a research scientist who did not see patients, he always kept his medical bag in the trunk of his car.

During the drive, he suddenly realized that he had forgotten to leave an important message for his secretary. Picking up his cellular phone, he called the office and managed to leave a partial message before he was out of range.

Traffic was moving slowly because of the steepness of the road. As he changed lanes, he saw a young boy, seven or eight years old and wearing a baseball cap, on the shoulder. He seemed to be watching the traffic. When the doctor's car drew close, he raised his thumb, indicating that he wanted a ride.

I don't pick up hitchhikers, the doctor said to himself. But something about the boy made him pull over.

"Where are you headed?" the doctor asked, when the boy was settled in the seat beside him.

No answer—just a serious look on his face and a restlessness that said he was anxious to get *somewhere.*

When the car came near an off ramp, the boy pulled on the doctor's sleeve and pointed. Message received, the doctor eased the car off the road. Moments later, he saw skid marks and a partially demolished guardrail. He stopped the car, ran to the railing, and looked down. A small school bus had rolled down the embankment and was lying on its side, its top crushed against a tree trunk.

Before he ran to help, the doctor tried his cellular phone. There was a dial tone! He called 911 and requested an ambulance.

Then, he grabbed his medical bag and some blankets from the car's trunk and went to work. The bus's rear emergency door was jammed, but with a burst of strength, he pulled it open. Before the ambulance arrived, he had removed all the children from the bus—all still alive—and done a brief exam of each one. He was able to tell the paramedics what sort of care each child would require.

"The driver is still in there," the doctor added.

A few minutes later, medics walked past him with a covered body on a stretcher.

"The driver?" he asked.

"No, it's another child. He was under the driver."

The doctor lifted the blanket and was shocked to discover his hitchhiker. The driver, one of the medics said, had apparently had a heart attack, and this boy had grabbed the wheel and probably kept the bus from

tumbling all the way to the floor of the canyon. His heroic act had cost him his life.

"But he's the one who brought me here!" the doctor insisted.

Back in his car, the doctor thought he had better call the resort and tell them that he was delayed. But the phone wasn't working. One of the highway patrolmen stopped by the car and told him not to bother with the phone; they were in the mountains, and too far from a transmitter. Then . . . how had he been able to reach 911 just a short while ago?

And was his hitchhiker real? He was beginning to wonder.

And then he found the boy's baseball cap, jammed between the front seats of the car.

It was a normal day in the life of a charter-boat captain: calm seas, sunshine, light breezes, and satisfied customers who, after many hours of fishing, were ready to head for shore.

So was the captain.

Captain Warren Gallop had been a Christian for many years. He was used to receiving God's "nudges"—indications that he needed to do something for his Father. On this day, God was definitely telling him to turn the boat around and head west.

His customers weren't happy with this turn of events. What *they* had in mind was a hot bath and a good dinner.

More than three miles later, Captain Gallop was beginning to feel foolish. What was he doing out here? Maybe he'd been following his own faulty intuition instead of the Holy Spirit's leading. He decided it was time to change course again and go home.

Taking one last look ahead, he found out why God had brought him here. Two young men were clinging to a raft, their strength to hold on nearly gone. The captain brought his boat alongside, and he and his passengers helped the weary castaways aboard.

"Our boat capsized about five hours ago," one of them said. "We've been trying to hang onto that raft ever since."

"We tried to swim to shore a couple of times," the other man said, "but we were going against the current, so we couldn't make any progress."

Back in the harbor, Captain Gallop helped each of his passengers onto the dock. Then he turned to ask the rescued men more questions about their ill-fated voyage. But they had disappeared.

It didn't matter. The captain had the satisfaction of knowing that when two of his fellow sailors were in deep trouble, God had used him to come miraculously to their rescue.

O Son of God, perform a miracle for me: change my heart. You, whose crimson blood redeems mankind, whiten my heart.

It is You Who make the sun bright and the ice sparkle; You Who make the rivers flow and the salmon leap.

Your skilled hand makes the nut tree blossom and the corn turn golden; Your Spirit composes the songs of the birds and the buzz of the bees.

Your creation is a million wondrous miracles, beautiful to behold. I ask of You just one more miracle: beautify my soul.

**— Celtic Prayer**
*The HarperCollins Book of Prayers*
Compiled by Robert Van de Weyer
San Francisco: Harper
1993

In those days Hezekiah became ill and was at the point of death. The prophet Isaiah son of Amoz went to him and said, "This is what the Lord says: Put your house in order, because you are going to die; you will not recover."

Hezekiah turned his face to the wall and prayed to the Lord, "Remember, O Lord, how I have walked before you faithfully and with wholehearted devotion and have done what is good in your eyes." And Hezekiah wept bitterly.

Then the word of the Lord came to Isaiah: "Go and tell Hezekiah, 'This is what the Lord, the God of your father David, says: I have heard your prayer and seen your tears; I will add fifteen years to your life. And I will deliver you and this city from the hand of the king of Assyria. I will defend this city.

"'This is the Lord's sign to you that the Lord will do what he has promised: I will make the shadow cast by the sun go back the ten steps it has gone down on the stairway of Ahaz.'" So the sunlight went back the ten steps it had gone down.

**— Isaiah 38:1-8 (NIV)**
*HOLY BIBLE*

A cancer inexplicably cured. A voice in a dream. A statue that weeps. A miracle is an event that strengthens faith. It is possible to look at most miracles and find a rational explanation in terms of natural cause and effect. It is possible to look at Rembrandt's Supper at Emmaus and find a rational explanation in terms of paint and canvas.

Faith in God is less apt to proceed from miracles than miracles from faith in God.

— **Frederich Buechner**
*Wishful Thinking —*
*A Seeker's ABC*

After Craig passed out and his pickup truck destroyed a couple of oleander bushes that had served as a highway divider and then veered across four lanes of traffic to come to a rest on the shoulder of the freeway . . . a passing motorist said it was a miracle that Craig's truck hadn't been involved in a major traffic accident.

When Craig was found before dawn lying face down near the fireplace in his home two weeks later, with no detectable heartbeat or sign of breathing . . . his wife said it was a miracle that she had awakened and found him, since she normally didn't rise until much later in the morning, and he was normally already at work by that hour.

When Craig arrived twenty minutes later at the hospital . . . the emergency room personnel said it was a miracle that the ambulance personnel had been wise enough not to attempt cardiopulmonary resuscitation, which most assuredly would have killed him.

When the various members of the foremost heart-surgery team in the region saw Craig in the hallway, and then immediately whirled about and returned to scrub for emergency surgery . . . the nurses said it was a miracle that the team was still in the hospital, since they were already several minutes late for their regularly scheduled weekly tee-off time at a local golf course.

When Craig's chest was opened and his aorta literally blew off his heart, and blood spewed on all in the room and even on the ceiling of the surgical theater . . . observing surgeons called it a miracle that the team was able to attach both heart and aorta to a blood pump within five seconds.

When Craig survived the five-hour surgery . . . the lead surgeon called it a miracle, since he had never seen a person survive an aortic aneurysm of that magnitude.

After Craig spent several days in intensive care, connected to a respirator and with a breathing tube prohibiting his ability to speak, showing very little signs of overall improvement . . . the coronary care unit nurses called it a miracle when his lungs began to function again and he was able to breathe without assistance, and without any sign of pneumonia.

When Craig was released from the hospital just eight days after his emergency heart surgery . . . the hospital personnel called it a miracle that he had recovered so quickly.

When Craig went fishing at his favorite mountain-stream fishing hole just two months later, something he had dreamed about in intensive care . . . his family called it a miracle.

So did Craig.

The Gentle Healer came into our town today.
He touched blind eyes and their darkness left to stay.
But more than the blindness, He took their sins away.
The Gentle Healer came into our town today.

The Gentle Healer came into our town today.
He spoke one word that was all He had to say.
And the one who had died just rose up straight away.
The Gentle Healer came into our town today.

Oh, He seems like just an ordinary man.
With dirty feet and rough but gentle hands.
But the words He says are hard to understand.
And yet He seems like just an ordinary man.

The Gentle Healer, He left our town today.
I just looked around and found He'd gone away.
Some folks from town who've followed Him, they say,
That the Gentle Healer is the Truth, the Life, the Way.

— **Michael Card**

When they arrived at the other side of the lake a demon-possessed man ran out from a graveyard, just as Jesus was climbing from the boat.

This man lived among the gravestones, and had such strength that whenever he was put into handcuffs and shackles — as he often was — he snapped the handcuffs from his wrists and smashed the shackles and walked away. No one was strong enough to control him. All day long and through the night he would wander among the tombs and in the wild hills, screaming and cutting himself with sharp pieces of stone.

When Jesus was still far out on the water, the man had seen him and had run to meet him, and fell down before him.

Then Jesus spoke to the demon within the man and said, "Come out, you evil spirit."

It gave a terrible scream, shrieking, "What are you going to do to me, Jesus, Son of the Most High God? For God's sake, don't torture me!"

"What is your name?" Jesus asked, and the demon replied, "Legion, for there are many of us here within this man."

Then the demons begged him again and again not to send them to some distant land.

Now as it happened there was a huge herd of hogs rooting around on the hill above the lake. "Send us into those hogs," the demons begged.

And Jesus gave them permission. Then the evil spirits came out of the man and entered the hogs, and the entire herd plunged down the steep hillside into the lake and drowned.

The herdsmen fled to the nearby towns and countryside, spreading the news as they ran. Everyone rushed out to see for themselves. And a large crowd soon gathered where Jesus was; but as they saw the man sitting there, fully clothed and perfectly sane, they were frightened. Those who saw what happened were telling everyone about it, and the crowd began pleading with Jesus to go away and leave them alone! So he got back into the boat. The man who had been possessed by the demons begged Jesus to let him go along. But Jesus said no.

"Go home to your friends," he told him, "and tell them what wonderful things God has done for you; and how merciful he has been."

So the man started off to visit the Ten Towns of that region and began to tell everyone about the great things Jesus had done for him; and they were awestruck by his story.

— **Mark 5:1-20 (TLB)**
*HOLY BIBLE*

In 1925, George was working for a foundry company. Not the safest job on earth. One day, a bit of molten iron got into his right eye and badly burned it. The scar that formed over the cornea virtually robbed him of his sight. The doctor who examined him said that the damage was permanent. There was no surgical procedure that could remove the scar.

More than twenty years later, George and his wife attended one of Evangelist Kathryn Kuhlman's healing services. Impressed by what they heard and saw, the Orrs attended several more services.

George would not have said that he put a lot of stock in divine healing. But during one of the meetings, he decided that it really was possible to be healed directly by God. He began to pray and ask God to heal his eye.

A few moments later, his eye began to tingle. Then it started to water; tears were pouring down his face. He was a little embarrassed, but he couldn't make it stop. Soon, the meeting was over and they were driving home.

That's when George realized what had happened. He could see clearly out of his right eye. The scar on his eye was gone. He returned to his original doctor two years later for an exam, and the doctor was amazed at what had

happened. The sort of scar tissue that had been on George's cornea doesn't dissolve or disappear that way.

The healing of George Orr's eye—even the doctor would have to admit—was a genuine miracle.

When you're sick, you need a doctor. When a doctor is sick, he needs a doctor, too. But as any doctor will tell you, medical care can't cure every ailment.

Dr. E. B. Henry is a prime example. In 1950, he was plagued by a painful sinus condition. A broken collarbone, suffered ten months earlier, had refused to heal normally; there was now a fleshy lump under his skin at the spot where the bone had broken. Dr. Henry also had near-total deafness in one ear.

"Let's go to one of Kathryn Kuhlman's healing services," his wife said one day. The doctor wasn't the least bit interested, but he agreed to go for his wife's sake.

The service was good theatre, Dr. Henry thought, but not much else. Then it got interesting. Miss Kuhlman started describing people in the audience and the healings they were receiving at that moment. Looking at the Henrys' section of the temple, she said something about a sinus opening up...hearing being restored in someone's ear . . . a lump dissolving . . . and the one being healed, she added, was a man.

Mrs. Henry knew that her husband was the man in question, but Dr. Henry would not stand and be recognized. He still wasn't sure he believed any of this stuff.

But it's hard to argue with a miracle. On the drive home, the doctor could now hear and breathe normally. His collarbone didn't heal instantly, but did heal properly a short time later.

Does God still heal today? You might want to ask a doctor.

Little boys should be outside riding their bikes, or playing baseball, or climbing trees. They shouldn't have to become familiar with doctors' offices or hospital rooms.

Nine-year-old Kevin was in danger of that very thing. Severe headaches sent him to the doctor's, where a CAT scan showed a large and deadly brain tumor. Steroids were prescribed to help bring down swelling in his brain, but no other treatment was given.

"Bring him back in two months and we'll do another scan," the doctor told Kevin's mother, Karen.

"In two months, the tumor will be gone," Karen told the doctor confidently. She believed that with persistent prayer, her son would be healed.

And so, for two months, Kevin's family, church deacons, church members, and people in their community stormed heaven with prayers for Kevin's full recovery.

In these situations, it's natural to have some doubts . . . to wonder if God is allowing an illness in order to accomplish some higher purpose. But Kevin's parents decided to put all doubts aside and trust Jesus. Their faith was a strong witness to Kevin, who also firmly believed that God would heal him.

The day came for the second CAT scan. The doctor was more than a little surprised when the scan showed absolutely no trace of the tumor.

"I can't explain it," he said. "Kevin received no treatment that would have destroyed the tumor—no radiation of any kind. All he had was prayer. And tumors of this type don't just disappear."

But Kevin's did.

Why, who makes much of a miracle?
As for me I know of nothing else but miracles,
Whether I walk the streets of Manhattan . . .
Or watch honey-bees busy around the hive of a
    summer forenoon,
Or animals feeding in the fields,
Or birds, or the wonderfulness of insects in the air,
Or the wonderfulness of the sundown, or of stars
    shining so quiet and bright,
Or the exquisite, delicate, thin curve of the new moon
    in spring . . .
To me every hour of the light and dark is a miracle,
Every cubic inch of space is a miracle,
Every square yard of the surface of the earth is spread
    with the same . . .
To me the sea is a continual miracle,
The fishes that swim—the rocks—the motion of the
    waves—the ships with men in them,
What stranger miracles are there?

— **Walt Whitman**
*From "Miracles," in Leaves of Grass*

My friend and I arrived at the convention center at 3:30 in the afternoon to find the place bustling with people eager to locate seats. If we had been a half hour later, no seats in the lower sections of the hall would have been available. By five o'clock, all 22,000 seats of the arena were filled. The healing service wasn't scheduled to begin until 7:30 that night.

And yet . . .

At 3:45, just minutes after we had settled into our seats, we noticed three people praying for a woman who was standing just four rows below us. Suddenly she gently, quietly, and peacefully slumped to the floor. When she stood again a few moments later, she suddenly took off running across the convention hall floor, obviously able to do something she had not been able to do before! A great shout of joy and applause rose from several who had watched the team pray for her. When she returned to her seat, she stood for two or three minutes, her arms raised in silent surrender, tears streaming down her cheeks, and then a great shout of praise burst from her lips, too.

A woman in a walker immediately stood and requested prayer. She, too, felt strong enough after prayer not only to run back and forth across the convention center floor, but to carry her walker over her head as she ran!

Perhaps inspired by what he saw, a man made his way down the steps next to us, with the help of his wife. Ashen in color and unsure of his step, he paused on each level of the risers, seemingly to gain strength for his next step. His wife carried his portable respirator, which was connected to the man's nostrils by small clear tubing. After several minutes of receiving prayer, he removed the tubing from his nose, took three massive breaths — and before our eyes, the color began to flow into his cheeks. He then started to move, and within seconds, he also was scurrying across the convention floor. This time, an even greater number of people in our section gave thanks to God. Without the respirator and with an ever-increasing liveliness in his steps, he eventually circled the entire lower floor of the convention hall before returning to his seat.

My friend leaned to me at that point and said, "The service isn't supposed to start for three more hours . . . but I guess God didn't know that."

Those who had prayed for the sick that afternoon remain nameless to us. So, too, are those who received healing miracles in their bodies. Names are not important. The work of God is what lingers in our memories.

My friend and I drove away from the healing meeting at 11:30 that night with this firm conclusion: wherever

two or more are gathered in the Lord's name, He is there in the midst.  Whenever two or more agree in prayer, with the full force of their faith believing for God to work, He does.  Whenever and wherever people touch other people in the name of Jesus, miracles happen.

— **An eyewitness account of events at a Benny Hinn meeting**

Marvin, a California businessman, had his first heart attack at the age of forty-six. After two more heart attacks, his physician told him either to sell his business or get a new doctor. Mr. Bird sold his business and moved, but his heart disease went with him. He continued to have recurring chest pains. Over a period of sixteen years, he was hospitalized for his heart condition seventeen times.

Late in 1970, Marvin's cardiologist sent him to a Veterans Administration Hospital to have a heart catheterization and coronary angiographic study. A few months later he had a coronary angiogram. The procedures revealed a complete occlusion of one of his coronary arteries and a 50 percent occlusion of the other two. The doctors recommended that he have coronary artery bypass surgery. Marvin refused, however, fearful that he wouldn't live through the surgery. His condition steadily declined. His chest pains grew worse and his body grew weaker.

Finally, two years later, Marvin permitted the cardiologists to operate, believing that if he didn't have the surgery, he wouldn't live long anyway. At the time, he was in near constant pain, and on a wide variety of heart-

regulating medications, routinely taking nitroglycerin, painkillers, and prescription narcotics. He did not have enough strength to lift himself out of a chair without assistance.

In the days before his scheduled surgery, Marvin had two vivid dreams. One night he dreamed that he saw his deceased father and brother-in-law coming over a hill toward him, beckoning him to join them. His second dream was about securing an apartment for a cousin who lived out of state. The apartment number, 315, stood out dramatically in his memory of the dream.

The next day, November 19, 1972, at precisely 3:15 in the afternoon, Marvin was suddenly and completely healed of his heart problems during a healing service held by Kathryn Kuhlman at the Shrine Auditorium in Los Angeles, California. He had no bodily sensation prior to his restoration to health and strength. Rather, when asked to stand, he found that he could stand — something previously impossible for him to do.

Nobody touched Marv. Nobody prayed for him directly. He had no unusual spiritual experience and no sense of the healing that was taking place in his body. He simply found he could do what he hadn't been able to do.

Marvin walked from the Shrine Auditorium several hours later pushing his wheelchair, his friends chasing him to try to keep up. He took his wife out to dinner that night and found that he had a vigorous appetite, something he hadn't had in a long time. He stayed up until past midnight, slept soundly, and awoke without pain.

Three days later he saw his physician, who commented immediately, "Why, Marv, what's happened? You look wonderful!" The doctor examined him, checked his records, took his pulse, shook his hand, and wished him a Merry Christmas.

Marvin and his wife attended church the next week and Marvin received Jesus Christ as his Savior. For the next three years, he spoke to numerous groups about his healing experience, and to his great joy, found that during some of these meetings, others were also healed.

J.W. was eighty years old when he went to the train station to pick up the young evangelist and his wife who were coming to speak at his church. As he drove to the place where they would be staying, he told them that eight months previously he had been diagnosed with an advanced stage of stomach cancer. He had tried all that medical science could offer him, but the physicians had eventually told him they had done all they knew to do, without any success. J.W. prayed in earnest that God would either heal him or take him to heaven. He was tired of living in pain, unable to eat anything other than liquified foods.

A few days after he prayed this heartfelt prayer, J.W. noticed that he didn't have any pain in his stomach. He felt greatly relieved, but was fearful at trying any solid foods. Then he received a letter from a friend who wrote, "The Bible says 'if they drink any deadly thing, it shall not hurt them.'* I'm believing that you can eat anything you want and it won't hurt you," the letter said. So J.W. took these words as assurance from God and he began to eat hearty meals.

He told the evangelist and his wife, "I got on the doctor's scales today and I've gained back all the weight

I lost with the cancer. I don't have any pain. I'm eating good meals. And if you ever need to tell the people that God still heals people, you can use me as your example!"

*Mark 16:18*

While Frank's mother was lying in a hospital, terminally ill and facing death, she suddenly began to sing the hymn "Blessed Assurance." She told her son later that she had not really wanted to sing, but somehow felt compelled to do so. As she sang, she heard a second voice joining with hers. As their voices blended in song, she felt great comfort. Frank's mother, however, had no idea where the other voice had come from. She had a private room and no doctor, nurse, or other hospital worker had been in her room at the time. "Who do you suppose was singing with me?" she asked her son. Frank intuitively responded, "It must have been the Lord."

When Frank told his wife about the incident his mother had relayed to him, she immediately recalled her devotional reading for that very day: "The Lord your God is with you, he is mighty to save. He will take great delight in you, he will quiet you with his love, he will rejoice over you with singing" (Zephaniah 3:17 NIV).

The skies around Milwaukee were boiling on the evening of July 17, 1981. Darrell, a member of the Republic Airlines ground crew, helped guide the plane to its docking point, lowered the stairway, and started up. Suddenly the sky lit up the airport as a bolt of lightning struck the tail of the plane. Darrell was knocked five feet into the air before slamming unconscious to the ground.

Rescue workers on the scene could find no pulse and CPR was begun immediately. In fact, Darrell had no pulse or heartbeat for nearly 45 minutes. But Teddy, an airline supervisor who rode in the ambulance with Darrell, began praying for him on the way to the hospital. "I sensed a miracle in the making," she said later. "I began to feel the presence of God in the ambulance."

Darrell was in critical condition when he reached the hospital. Immediately Darrell's family and friends began gathering at the hospital in a  prayer vigil. Eventually, more than eighty people were on site praying for him; the hospital staff assumed he was some sort of celebrity.

Before long, their presence and prayers began to have an unusual effect. Darrell's groans subsided into a quiet supplication which he repeated for hours: "Bless my soul, Lord."

The next morning he awoke completely restored in body but with a severe loss of memory. Pamela, his young wife, was hurt when he failed to recognize her. But she was devastated when he asserted that the baby she was carrying inside her must belong to someone else. As he fell asleep again, Pam prayed. Grateful that Darrell's life had been restored, Pamela now asked God to bring the "real" Darrell back to her and their child on the way.

As she continued to pray, suddenly Darrell stirred and awoke. "Hi, honey!" were his first words.

In her book, *One Woman's Liberation*, Shirley Boone tells of a miracle that became the turning point in the faith of her daughter, Lindy.

Lindy had been given a small mouse for Christmas by a friend who was also a mouse owner. The girls not only had dreams of breeding the mice for pet stores, but had become quite attached to them as pets.

While Shirley was out one day, a clearly distressed Lindy brought her listless mouse to her dad, entertainer Pat Boone. "Daddy," Lindy said, "can you take my little mouse to the vet right away?"

The idea of taking a mouse to the vet was so incongruous that Pat almost laughed. But looking at Lindy, he knew that the situation wasn't at all funny to her. After calling both the pet store and a vet, Pat knew there wasn't anything that either could do. "A sick mouse is a dead mouse" was the answer from both sources.

So Pat took Lindy, Laury (another daughter) and the mouse upstairs to pray for the mouse in the bedroom where the family had become accustomed to praying together. On the way, Pat's faith began to falter. "What if the Lord doesn't answer my prayer? What if the mouse dies while we're praying for it? What will that do to

Lindy's faith? If God doesn't take any interest in this mouse, it won't bother me. But how will Lindy react? She's so emotionally involved."

Even as these thoughts filled his mind, Pat began to pray. "Lord, we're not asking that a mountain be cast into the sea. This morning we're just asking that this little mouse recover. You made this little mouse, so You must care about it, just as You care about Lindy and Laury and me. We care about the mouse, but we can't do anything about it . . . and since we know You're concerned about every one of Your creatures and since Jesus promised that we might ask anything in His name, we believe that You will answer our prayer and help the little mouse."

As Pat then began to give thanks to God, the mouse twitched. Lindy placed the mouse on the bed and began crying. When she opened her eyes the little fellow was sitting up, rubbing his nose with his front paws. Over the next hour or so, he was able to take food and water and before long, he was friskier than ever.

As Pat and the girls joyfully watched the mouse recover that afternoon, Lindy began to sob again. "Now, what's the matter?" Pat wanted to know. Lindy began to explain how an older boy at school had begun to argue with her about her faith causing her to begin to doubt God's love for her. Lindy had talked directly to God about this and, in the process, had asked Him to "do something totally illogical to strengthen my faith. Please show me that You do exist and are listening to me and that this boy is wrong."

God had done more than heal Lindy's mouse that day. He had strengthened her faith.

One evening two young men who regularly attended the weekly Thursday-night prayer meeting at New York Avenue Presbyterian Church in Washington, D.C., noticed two men sitting just outside the partly opened door that led to the prayer meeting room. Thinking the shadowy figures were there to meet with the pastor (his study was just across the hall from where they sat) the two men went on into the prayer meeting and thought nothing more of their presence. The next week, however, they noticed the same two men sitting in the same positions. One of them sat in front of the other with his head tilted forward as if to listen intently. Their curiosity aroused, the young men decided to try to meet the two strangers after the service.

Then as they hurried from the room at the close of the prayer meeting, they found the men had gone. As they exited from the door near the pastor's study, they found fresh footprints in the snow. One of the young men exclaimed, "One of those men was Abraham Lincoln!" The other asked, "How do you know?" The first man replied, "Look at the size of that footprint. Lincoln has the largest feet in Washington!"

They briskly trotted toward the White House, arriving there just in time to see the tall, sad-eyed President and a Secret Service man entering the grounds. They raced back to the church to ask the pastor if he knew that President Lincoln had been at the prayer meeting the last two Thursday nights. The pastor told them that he knew of the visits, but begged them not to reveal President Lincoln's secret.

Years later, a historian found a letter from President Lincoln among the archives of that church. It stated that he had given due consideration to the question of salvation and was now ready to give a public confession of his faith in Jesus Christ. It also stated that he wished to be accepted for membership in the church the following Sunday, April 18. The letter was written on April 13, 1865.

Abraham Lincoln was assassinated on April 14, 1865.

I t is hard to escape the conclusion that many people have received through Christian prayer remarkable healings which bring glory to Christ and which are difficult or impossible to explain away in conventional medical terms. The available medical evidence and case histories indicate that the healings themselves have to be regarded as facts. Although some people might attempt to interpret those facts in a variety of ways, mounting evidence indicates that prayer in Christ's name seems to be an important factor in many medically inexplicable recoveries.

— **David C. Lewis**

*The Kingdom and the Power*  by  Gary S. Grieg and Kevin N. Springer, eds., copyright © 1993, Regal Books, Ventura, CA 93003.  Used by permission.

Does God change the course of nature when we pray? This is not a question to be decided by logic. It is a question of fact. It is ridiculous to ask whether God COULD change the usual course of nature, although science used to say the laws of nature could not be broken. Has He done so or hasn't He? If He does, He does. And it seems He does now as surely and perhaps as often as He did in Christ's day. Who of us have prayed without receiving some startling answer? You could not persuade most soldiers otherwise. Either our wars have produced more liars than you could count, or miracles have happened. Fish have jumped into boats, birds have landed on men's heads, and strange winds have blown boats to shore. . .

Let one story illustrate: it was written by Sergeant Johnny Bartek, a companion of Captain Eddie Rickenbacker:

As soon as we were in the rafts at the mercy of God, we realized that we were not in any condition to expect help from Him. We spent many hours of each day confessing our sins to one another and to God. . .

Then we prayed—and God answered. It was real. We needed water. We prayed for water and we got water—all we needed. Then we asked for fish, and we got fish. And we got meat when we prayed. Sea gulls don't go around sitting on people's heads waiting to be caught! On that eleventh day when those planes flew by, we all cried like babies. It was then I prayed again to God and said: "If you'll send that one plane back for us I promise I'll believe in You and tell everyone else." That plane came back and the others flew on. It just happened? It did not! God sent that plane back!

Our hard-headed psychologist would find it hard to explain all that by "mental radio." Telepathy might have called the pilot in the airplane and even the sea gulls, and the fish—but hardly the rain!

— **Frank C. Laubach**
Prayer: the Mightiest Force in the World
Westwood, NJ: Spire Books
1959

I t is important to understand that miracles are never given for the purpose of amazing, astounding, amusing, nor entertaining. They have a much more serious purpose than this and one compatible with the dignity and majesty of Deity. The vulgar and cheap displays of supernatural phenomena, as that witnessed at spiritist seances where trivial questions are asked and answered ("Where did I lose my gold watch?" "Should I invest in such and such stocks in Wall Street?" "Can I talk with my dead husband?"), oftimes a performance marked by horns floating in the air, voices coming from various directions, and in many instances outright fraud, all of which smacks of sorcery and the black arts, and leaves no doubt that such is not of God, but rather the work of depraved demon spirits.

**— James Gordon Lindsay**
All About the Gift of Working of Miracles
Dallas, TX: The Voice of Healing
Publishing Co., 1963

How do we pray for someone in need when we don't even know a need exists? If we are in tune with the Holy Spirit, He will tell us when and who to pray for.

During World War II, a young pilot named Edgar flew transport planes in the Philippines. Late one night, his wife Elizabeth awoke and somehow knew that she had to pray for her husband — and pray hard and immediately. Her prayer lasted nearly an hour. Finally, she felt a calm in her spirit and she was able to stop praying and fall back asleep.

Two weeks later, she received a letter from Edgar telling her how he had been flying a routine mission when he was caught in an unexpected tropical storm. The winds of the storm had been so fierce, the wings of his airplane seemed to be "flapping" as he watched them from his cockpit window. He was barely able to keep the plane on an even keel. By the time he had managed to return to the base, the fuel gauge on his plane registered empty. The battle with the winds had lasted almost an hour . . . at the exact time his wife had awakened and begun to pray.

Both Edgar and his wife knew that God had intervened sovereignly on Edgar's behalf, and that Elizabeth's prayers had been a part of God's plan for that hour.

In the 1930s, Stalin ordered the purge of all Bibles and all believers. In Stavropol, Russia, this order was carried out with a vengeance. Thousands of Bibles were confiscated and multitudes of believers were sent to the gulags where most died for being "enemies of the state." Years later a team was sent to Stavropol. The city's history wasn't known at the time. But when the team was having difficulty getting Bibles shipped from Moscow, someone mentioned the existence of a warehouse outside town where the original confiscated Bibles had been stored since Stalin's day. After much prayer by the team, one member finally got up the courage to go to the warehouse and ask the officials if the Bibles were still there. Sure enough, they were. Then he asked if they could be removed and distributed again to the people of Stavropol. The answer was "yes."

The next day the team returned with a truck and several Russian helpers to load the Bibles. One of the helpers was a young man—a skeptical, agnostic, hostile collegian who had come only for a day's wages. As they were loading Bibles, one member of the team noticed that the young man had disappeared. Eventually they found him in the corner of the warehouse weeping. He had slipped away hoping secretly to take a Bible for himself. What he found inside shook him to the core.

The inside page of the Bible he picked up had the handwritten signature of his grandmother! It was her personal Bible. Of the thousands of Bibles still left in that warehouse, he stole the very one belonging to his grandmother—a woman persecuted for her faith all her life.

**As told by Elaine Griffith,**
International School Project
San Clemente, California

# Miracles are not contrary to nature but only contrary to what we know about nature.

**— St. Augustine of Hippo**
*Draper's Book of Quotations
for the Christian World*

One day a Christian believer in Siberia had a most unusual dream. He was told to go to Moscow where he would find a Bible for the church he attended. The man resisted the idea at first, knowing that Moscow's churches had precious few Bibles of their own. But the dream had seemed so vivid and authoritative. And he kept thinking of his 150 fellow church members without a single copy of Scripture among them. So the man set out on a journey two thousand miles across the tundra.

About that time another believer, known as Brother Andrew, and his companion Hans, drove their VW from Holland down through Poland, crossed the border into Russia at Brest, and traveled on seven hundred miles to Moscow. Soon after arriving in the city the two men decided to check out the midweek service at a certain Baptist church. They hoped to make contacts there so they could unload some hot merchandise. Andrew and Hans had managed to maneuver past border check points and prying guards with a load of Russian Bibles tucked away in their car.

But distributing the Bibles was as risky as slipping them through the Iron Curtain. It's not like you could advertise. And one never knew who might be a KGB informant in a

church, or even if the pastor was under pressure to report everything.

So when Andrew and Hans walked into the Thursday night meeting carrying a sample Russian Bible, they had a plan. After the service the two lingered in the vestibule checking out the twelve hundred worshipers milling past. Each man prayed separately that God would direct him to someone they could safely entrust with their smuggled Scriptures.

Soon Andrew spotted a thin, balding man in his forties standing against the wall. He felt a familiar "moment of recognition." The directive to talk to the man seemed very clear, but Andrew waited for Hans to inch over towards him. Before Andrew could speak, his companion said, "I've spotted our man!" In that vestibule crowded with hundreds of people Hans nodded toward the worshiper Andrew had chosen.

With hearts thumping they walked up to the stranger and attempted to introduce themselves and explain where they'd come from. He only stared at them, perplexed, until he caught the word "Dutch." It turned out he spoke German. So the three began a vigorous conversation in that language.

Andrew and Hans listened incredulously as the man told his story. This was the believer who'd come all the way from Siberia to find a Bible for his church, hoping against hope that God would somehow come through on the dream. Hans had the privilege of delivering the good news: "You were told to come eastward for two thousand miles to get a Bible, and we were told to go westward two thousand miles carrying Bibles to churches in Russia. And here we meet tonight, recognizing each other the instant we meet."

King Herod got it into his head to go after some of the church members. He murdered James, John's brother. When he saw how much it raised his popularity ratings with the Jews, he arrested Peter—all this during Passover Week, mind you—and had him thrown in jail, putting four squads of four soldiers each to guard him. He was planning a public lynching after Passover.

All the time that Peter was under heavy guard in the jailhouse, the church prayed for him most strenuously.

Then the time came for Herod to bring him out for the kill. That night, even though shackled to two soldiers, one on either side, Peter slept like a baby. And there were guards at the door keeping their eyes on the place. Herod was taking no chances!

Suddenly there was an angel at his side and light flooding the room. The angel shook Peter and got him up: "Hurry!" The handcuffs fell off his wrists. The angel said, "Get dressed. Put on your shoes." Peter did it. Then, "Grab your coat and let's get out of here." Peter followed him, but didn't believe it was really an angel—he thought he was dreaming.

Past the first guard and then the second, they came to the iron gate that led into the city. It swung open before them on its own, and they were out on the street, free as the breeze. At the first intersection the angel left him, going his own way. That's when Peter realized it was no dream. "I can't believe it—this really happened! The Master sent His angel and rescued me from Herod's vicious little production and the spectacle the Jewish mob was looking forward to."

Still shaking his head, amazed, he went to Mary's house, the Mary who was John Mark's mother. The house was packed with praying friends. When he knocked on the door to the courtyard, a young woman named Rhoda came to see who it was. But when she recognized his voice—Peter's voice!—she was so excited and eager to tell everyone Peter was there that she forgot to open the door and left him standing in the street.

But they wouldn't believe her, dismissing her, dismissing her report. "You're crazy," they said. She stuck by her story, insisting. They still wouldn't believe her and said, "It must be his angel." All this time poor Peter was standing out in the street, knocking away.

Finally they opened up and saw him—and went wild! Peter put his hands up and calmed them down. He described how the Master had gotten him out of jail, then said, "Tell James and the brothers what's happened." He left them and went off to another place.

At daybreak the jail was in an uproar. "Where is Peter? What's happened to Peter?" When Herod sent for him and they could neither produce him nor explain why not, he ordered their execution: "Off with their heads!" Fed up with Judea and Jews, he went for a vacation to Caesarea.

— **Eugene H. Peterson,** Navpress, 1993

Music, it is said, has charms to soothe the savage beast. In God's hands, it can be a weapon of war.

After forty years in the desert, the Israelites had finally reached the Promised Land. Joshua circumcised the new generation, as the Lord commanded. This was done at their camp in Gilgal, on the plains of Jericho. Gilgal is also where the Israelites had their first meal from the land; God stopped sending manna (bread from heaven) the very next day.

The people of Jericho knew the Israelites were coming, and they were determined to keep them out of the city. God, however, had decided to deliver Jericho into the Israelites' hands.

Joshua was the leader of God's people. He was given these orders:

March once around the city with all the armed men. Do that for six days. Have seven priests carry trumpets of rams' horns in front of the ark of the covenant. On the seventh day, march around the city seven times, and tell the priests to blow those trumpets! When you hear them sound a long blast, tell all the people to give a loud shout. That's when the wall of the city will collapse. Then you can all go in.

What an unusual battle plan! But it worked. Once again, God showed His people that when they obey His Word, He works in a marvelous way.

**— Based on Joshua 5-6:20**

My God can do anything, anything,
   yes, anything.
My God can do anything, yes, anything.

He made the earth with all its fullness
And all that time shall bring.

My God can do anything, yes, anything.
My God controls the wind and weather
He sends the sunshine and the rain.
He holds this universe together
With love He rules His great domain
He understands each little heartache
He even knows the pain you bear
And He will never get too busy
To give an answer to your prayer.

— **Vep Ellis**

Earthquakes, mudslides, floods—living in California can be a real adventure. As scary as (or scarier than) those three "events," however, is a wildfire. High temperatures, high winds, and a lack of rain can create a dangerous situation.

Gary and his wife, Angela, were living in their new home in the hills around Los Angeles. One day, a raging fire sprang up near their neighborhood. The fire department evacuated everyone in the area, but Gary wouldn't leave. He was determined to fight fire with . . . a garden hose, if necessary.

Entertainer Pat Boone, one of Gary's friends from church, tried to call and ask how things were going. After three tries and three sets of busy signals, Pat called the operator and was told that the lines were down in Gary's neighborhood. But Pat was determined to reach him, so he prayed and tried again. This time, the phone rang and Gary answered.

Pat told him that their Sunday school class was praying for him and his home's safety.

"You're praying too, aren't you, Gary?"

"God's busy," was the essence of his response. "I don't want to bother Him with something like this."

"But you belong to Jesus, and everything you own belongs to Him. Can't you pray and ask Him to watch out for what is His?"

Gary saw the logic in that and agreed to pray. People at church continued to pray, too.

The result? The fire destroyed houses and land on three sides of Gary and Angela's place . . . but did not touch their house or property.

# MIRACLES
## ARE HEAVEN SENT

The world is like a bright display of miracles galore,
And daily I discover even more.
The bird in flight,
the dawn of day,
the mighty ocean's roar,
And far away new places to explore.
But all these wonders, great or small,
are more reflections of the greatest wonder of them all,
The wonder of His love.
He spoke a word and set the starry firmament in place,
But for our life He gave His own, O Miracle of Grace.

— **Ralph Carmichael**

*Miracle of Grace* by Ralph Carmichael, appeared in *He's Everything to Me Plus 103* compiled by Ralph Carmichael, copyright © 1985, Adm. by EMI Christian Music Publishing. Used by permission.

Lydia awoke at 1 a.m., startled by a voice she thought was saying to, "Pray for Gordon." She rationalized to herself that she must have been dreaming about Gordon — a young man from their church who had gone halfway across the country to attend seminary — and that surely he didn't need her prayers since he was a good man and God would take care of him. So Lydia snuggled back into her bed and tried to sleep. But she heard the voice again as if calling to her from an adjacent room. She got up, found nobody in the next room, and returned to bed. By this time, her husband Robert was awake and she told him what had prompted her to get up. He advised, "Oh, you probably ate too much supper last night. Gordon's all right." Lydia tried to sleep, but could not. Finally, she got up and knelt down beside their bed to pray. As soon as her knees hit the floor, she felt several severe pains grip her head. She cried out as the pain struck her and her cry awoke Robert. He quickly got up to join her in prayer. As he knelt, he, too, felt severe shooting pains in his head. The two clasped hands and began to pray fervently for Gordon. In about ten minutes the pain subsided in both of them and they returned to bed and quickly fell asleep.

Two weeks later they heard from their young friend Gordon that he had been suffering with a migraine headache for nearly a week before the end of the school term. Trying desperately to study for his final exams, he had experienced such intense pain that his eyes wouldn't focus and nausea wracked his body. He wrote that the pain had become so intense one night about 1 a.m. that he had thought he would need to go to the hospital. Then, he wrote, about half an hour later the pain left his head instantly and completely. He felt a strong sense of God's presence. He went to sleep and slept peacefully for the first time in a week, awaking refreshed and able to take his exams without any ill effects.

In his letter, Gordon gave praise to God for healing him. Upon receiving his letter, Lydia and Robert did the same!

A friend of mine, whose wife died tragically and suddenly, almost went out of his mind with shock and grief. His doctors recommended a trip abroad, and he went to Italy. But travel was not the answer, and one day he climbed a famous mountain pass with a single thought in mind. He was going to commit suicide.

As he stood at the edge of the precipice, ready to jump, he suddenly heard music. At the edge of a cave, by the side of the mountain path, a barefoot lad was playing a harmonica.

"I had felt completely alone," my friend told me afterward, "all reason stifled by the depth of my grief. But somehow that music, so pure and simple and unexpected in that wild place—somehow it got through to me. It made me realize how much beauty and goodness life still had to offer—and how ungrateful and selfish I was being in my grief. It proved to me that when you need a miracle most, God will be with you, standing by, ready to reach out and touch you with His hand."

—**Olive Bradshaw**
*The Guideposts Treasury of Hope*
p. 26

My Father is omnipotent,
And that you can't deny,
A God of might and miracles
'Tis written in the sky.

Though here His glory has been shown;
We still can't fully see
The wonders of His might, His throne;
'Twill take eternity.

The Bible tells us of His pow'r
And wisdom all way through;
And ev'ry little bird and flow'r
Are testimonies, too.

(Chorus)
It took a miracle to put the stars in place.
It took a miracle to hang the world in space.
But when He saved my soul, cleansed and made me
        whole,
It took a miracle of love and grace.

— **John W. Peterson**
*Hill and Range Songs, Inc., 1948*

We are tempted to ask God to act miraculously to meet our wants on our timetable—and according to our specifications. Satan tempts us with impatience with God and His providence. The Lord is more concerned about our real needs than He is about our wants. What He denies us or delays is always to get us to the place where what we want is what He knows we need. He will never give us anything which will be a shortcut to realizing the miracle of our own cross and resurrection.

The secret of the abundant life is death to ourselves and regeneration through a personal experience of the uplifting power of the resurrection. A person who lives in the ambiance of that transforming miracle is not constantly demanding evidences that the Lord is able. And the amazing thing is that his life is a succession of serendipities of miraculous interventions. But not according to his demand or agenda. Jesus astonished people by His mighty works, not because He demanded that God act for the validation of His ministry or His own assurance. Rather, He was in complete harmony with the Father's plan and purpose.

— **Lloyd J. Ogilvie**

111

We see Jesus as He takes the lunch—five barley loaves and two small fishes. The Bible says, first, He gave thanks for it. Second, the Bible says, He broke it.

A scientific question emerges, "Is Jesus releasing the atoms that are in the bread?" It's a very serious question. How is Jesus doing this? They say that in one little pound of coal there is enough heat stored up to heat an entire city, if we could learn how to release the atoms in it. Our scientists discovered how to split the atom and to cause a chain reaction. Then they created a monster bomb that leveled two cities in Japan. Today there are thousands and thousands of these bombs held by America, Russia, France, England, China, India, and possibly other nations. We are scared to death. We are frightened of these unholy instruments of death.

On the other hand, the scientists are saying that the same atom power which can be released for evil can be released for good. Is Jesus now releasing the atoms in a few pieces of bread and a few pieces of fish? Is this a miracle, or is it another work of the Father? Is Jesus just simply doing what He knows to do with what He created?

Jesus gave thanks. Then He broke the bread. He handed it to His disciples and as He handed it out it never

diminished. Every time He gave a handful, there was another handful for a disciple to take and to hand out.

Was this a release of atoms? Was it a scientific breakthrough? Is it time for our scientists to catch up with God's own miracle-working power? Do we have to face the threat of a hungry world and worry ourselves to death about overpopulation? Not if we believe in God . . . not if we have faith. The population may become so huge it's uncountable but if we become like a little child and have faith in God, there will be a way for every man to eat. There are so many without jobs that it seems like there will never be enough, but the man who practices Seed-Faith and the woman who practices Seed-Faith operates on a higher level. And he or she will be taken care of. I believe that, I know that.

— **Oral Roberts**

*Miracles Of Christ* by Oral Roberts, copyright ©
1975, Pinoak Publications, Tulsa, OK.

The widow of Zarephath was a desperate woman. There hadn't been any rain in ages and her pantry was empty. The day came when she knew that her life was going to end. So, she went to the town gate and began gathering sticks for a fire to cook one last meal.

Who should come along but the prophet Elijah. In a way, he was partly responsible for her troubles. God had decided to punish the new king of Israel, Ahab, for his insistence on worshipping Baal, a false god. The punishment? No dew or rain in Israel for what turned out to be three-and-a-half years (Luke 4:25). The man who brought Ahab God's message? Elijah.

But God is also compassionate. He brought Elijah to the widow to work some miracles.

Elijah asked her for some water, which she provided. Then he asked for the impossible: a piece of bread.

"All I have is a handful of flour and a tiny bit of oil," she said. "I was just going home to cook one last meal for my son and myself, and then we will surely die."

"Not so fast," Elijah said. "Go make a small cake for me, and then make some for you and your son. God has told me that the flour and the oil will not run out until this drought is over."

To her credit, the woman was obedient and trusting. And the oil and flour lasted and lasted.

God wasn't through. One day the woman's son became very sick and died. Here is where the woman began to doubt God. But Elijah didn't. He placed the boy's body on his bed, stretched himself out on the boy three times, and asked God to restore his life. And God did.

The woman's doubts were gone. "Now I know you are a man of God," she told Elijah, "and that when you give the word of the Lord, you are speaking the truth." Nothing settles the issue like a miracle.

**— Based on 1 Kings 16:29-17:24**

Vic wanted to do the right thing. He wasn't rich, but he made a decision to give a small percentage of his paycheck to help people who were less fortunate.

Things were going along just fine. Then, Vic's family had some financial difficulties. Vic was sorely tempted to stop giving away that small part of his income. But instead, he said a prayer and asked God for reassurance, for some sort of sign that his family would be okay.

A week later, he pulled into a gas station to fill his car's tank — something he did every Saturday. A full tank normally lasted just one week.

Suddenly, Vic realized that God had given him the comfort he'd prayed for. You see, Vic had done the same amount of driving as usual, but he had forgotten to fill the gas tank the previous Saturday. His car had operated for an additional seven days on...air? Or a prayer?

After the apostles returned to Jesus and reported what they had done, he slipped quietly away with them toward the city of Bethsaida. But the crowds found out where he was going, and followed. And he welcomed them, teaching them again about the Kingdom of God and curing those who were ill.

Late in the afternoon all twelve of the disciples came and urged him to send the people away to the nearby villages and farms, to find food and lodging for the night. "For there is nothing to eat here in this deserted spot," they said.

But Jesus replied, "You feed them!"

"Why, we have only five loaves of bread and two fish among the lot of us," they protested; "or are you expecting us to go and buy enough for this whole mob?" For there were about 5,000 men there!

"Just tell them to sit down on the ground in groups of about fifty each," Jesus replied. So they did.

Jesus took the five loaves and two fish and looked up into the sky and gave thanks; then he broke off pieces for his disciples to set before the crowd. And everyone ate and ate; still, twelve basketfuls of scraps were picked up afterwards!

— **Luke 9:10-17 (TLB)**
*HOLY BIBLE*

Some people (kids especially) might not consider it a good thing when meatloaf lasts longer than expected. But when you have nineteen people to feed, it's a real blessing.

Back in the 1960s, a small prayer community in Michigan had separate homes for men and women, and a common dining room. The pantry was never filled to overflowing, but there was always food. Visitors were welcomed with open arms.

Each member took a turn preparing meals. One evening, one of the women went to the refrigerator and was greeted by a lonely two-pound package of ground beef. With a lot of filler, it would just barely make enough meatloaf for the twelve of them.

Naturally, the unexpected happened. A carload of young men, fresh from a retreat in Massachusetts, pulled up after an 800-mile drive. Who could turn them away?

The woman put extra bread on the table and mixed up more fruit drink. And then they all did some serious praying.

Somehow, nineteen people each had a helping of that meatloaf. When it came time for seconds, they were a little surprised to discover that half of the meatloaf was still available. Some even had thirds, and still there was half a meatloaf on the platter. Enough meatloaf remained to provide sandwiches for the next day's lunch!

The selfsame net, and the selfsame lake,
And it seemed there was nothing left to take;
But the Master said, "Let down your net!"
What happened the world can never forget—
Ah, the story thrills us even yet!
So many the fish, yet the net did not break.

Thus spake the Master — "The right side try";
And the men who had watched the night go by
With never a fish for their patient quest,
With never an hour for needed rest,
Gave heed at once to their Lord's behest,
And the miracle saw — the great supply!

When blessings seem scarce, and growing less,
And our trying results in fruitlessness,
A right side still is surely at hand,
If the heart, attent for the Lord's command,
But follow the course that He has planned,
Ah, then shall we see how His hand can bless.

**— William M. Runyan**
*"The Right Side"*

The miracles, in fact, are a retelling in small letters of the very same story which is written across the whole world in letters too large for some of us to see.

— **C. S. Lewis**
*God in the Dock*

I read in the Bible the promise of God,
That nothing for Him is too hard;
Impossible things He has promised to do
If we faithfully trust in His Word.

The Word of the Lord is an anchor secure
When winds of uncertainty blow;
Though man in his weakness may falter and fail,
His Word will not fail us, we know.

Creator of all things with infinite pow'r,
He spoke—they appeared by His mouth;
Impossible things are not known unto Him,
He made us, He ruleth the earth.

(Chorus)

Nothing is impossible when you put your trust in God;
Nothing is impossible when you're trusting in His Word.
Hearken to the voice of God to thee:
"Is there anything too hard for me?"
Then put your trust in God alone and rest upon His Word;
For ev'rything, O ev'rything, yes ev'rything is possible with
God!

— **Eugene L. Clark**
*Best of Favorites Songbook, Vol. 2*
Benson Music, 1993

And thou shalt take this rod in thine hand, wherewith thou shalt do signs (Exodus 4:17).

When God Almighty linked Himself to that rod, it was worth more than all the armies the world had ever seen. Look and see how that rod did its work. It brought up the plagues of flies, and the thunderstorm, and turned the water into blood. It was not Moses, however, nor Moses' rod that did the work, but it was the God of the rod, the God of Moses. As long as God was with him, he could not fail.

**— D. L. Moody**
*The D. L. Moody Year Book Selected by* Emma Moody Fitt, New York: Fleming H. Revell

The Israelites were a thorn in Pharaoh's side. He was determined to get rid of them. When his plan to kill all their newborn boys failed, he settled for enslaving them.

God heard His people's cries and sent Moses to their rescue. First, God wanted Moses to go to Israel's elders and let them know that he, Moses, had been sent to bring about their deliverance.

Moses had doubts about what God could do. "What if my fellow Israelites don't believe I saw You?" he asked God.

"Throw your staff on the ground," God said. It became a snake! "Pick it up by the tail," God said. It became a staff again! As a further sign to show the people, God said, "Put your hand inside your cloak." When Moses brought his hand back out, it was white with leprosy. "Do it again," God said. This time, his hand came out with no sign of disease.

Pharaoh was another hard case, but God had purposely hardened his heart. He wanted to make sure that the Egyptians knew who He was—the one true God—when He finally freed the Israelites.

Each time Pharaoh refused to let the people go, God sent another sign. First, He turned all the water in Egypt into blood. Then He sent a plague of frogs. Then He caused the dust of the ground to turn into gnats. Then He sent swarms of flies everywhere (except Goshen, where His people lived). Then He put a plague on Egyptian livestock.

There was more! God caused boils to form on all Egyptian men and animals. Then He sent a hailstorm—to Egypt, not Goshen. An infestation of locusts came next, followed by three days of total darkness (everywhere except where the Israelites lived). Finally, God said, "Enough!" The last sign was the plague on every first-born in Egypt, be it human or livestock. The Israelites, following Moses' and his brother Aaron's instructions, prepared themselves for what was to become the first Passover—and their firstborns' lives were spared. Not so the Egyptians.

Pharaoh finally let the Israelites go, but then he changed his mind. God parted the waters of the Red Sea so that the Israelites could cross in safety. As the Egyptians tried to follow, God closed the waters and drowned the entire army.

There were more miracles beyond the sea—bitter water became sweet after God told Moses to throw a piece of wood into it. God sent manna—bread from heaven—six days a week to feed His people.

So, were the Israelites overwhelmed by all these signs and wonders? Grateful? Convinced of God's faithfulness? Not always. But who among us today is not encouraged when we read about the amazing steps God took to show His great love for His children—freeing them from bondage and putting them on a road to a Land of Promise.

**— Based on Exodus 1-16**

Now the time came for the Lord to take Elijah to heaven—by means of a whirlwind! Elijah said to Elisha as they left Gilgal, "Stay here, for the Lord has told me to go to Bethel."

But Elisha replied, "I swear to God that I won't leave you!"

So they went on together to Bethel. There the young prophets of Bethel Seminary came out to meet them and asked Elisha, "Did you know that the Lord is going to take Elijah away from you today?"

"Quiet!" Elisha snapped. "Of course I know it."

Then Elijah said to Elisha, "Please stay here in Bethel, for the Lord has sent me to Jericho."

But Elisha replied again, "I swear to God that I won't leave you." So they went on together to Jericho.

Then the students at Jericho Seminary came to Elisha and asked him, "Do you know that the Lord is going to take away your master today?"

"Will you please be quiet?" he commanded. "Of course I know it!"

Then Elijah said to Elisha, "Please stay here, for the Lord has sent me to the Jordan River."

But Elisha replied as before, "I swear to God that I won't leave you."

So they went on together and stood before the Jordan River as fifty of the young prophets watched from a distance. Then Elijah folded his cloak together and struck the water with it; and the river divided and they went across on dry ground!

When they arrived on the other side Elijah said to Elisha, "What wish shall I grant you before I am taken away?"

And Elisha replied, "Please grant me twice as much prophetic power as you have had."

"You have asked a hard thing," Elijah replied. "If you see me when I am taken from you, then you will get your request. But if not, then you won't."

As they were walking along, talking, suddenly a chariot of fire, drawn by horses of fire, appeared and drove between them, separating them, and Elijah was carried by a whirlwind into heaven.

Elisha saw it and cried out, "My father! My father! The Chariot of Israel and the charioteers!"

As they disappeared from sight he tore his robe. Then he picked up Elijah's cloak and returned to the bank of the Jordan River, and struck the water with it.

"Where is the Lord God of Elijah?" he cried out. And the water parted and Elisha went across!

When the young prophets of Jericho saw what had happened, they exclaimed, "The spirit of Elijah rests upon

Elisha!" And they went to meet him and greeted him respectfully.

"Sir," they said, "just say the word and fifty of our best athletes will search the wilderness for your master; perhaps the Spirit of the Lord has left him on some mountain or in some ravine."

"No," Elisha said, "don't bother."

But they kept urging until he was embarrassed, and finally said, "All right, go ahead." Then fifty men searched for three days, but didn't find him.

Elisha was still at Jericho when they returned. "Didn't I tell you not to go?" he growled.

Now a delegation of the city officials of Jericho visited Elisha. "We have a problem," they told him. "This city is located in beautiful natural surroundings, as you can see; but the water is bad, and causes our women to have miscarriages."

"Well," he said, "bring me a new bowl filled with salt." So they brought it to him.

Then he went out to the city well and threw the salt in and declared, "The Lord has healed these waters. They shall no longer cause death or miscarriage."

And sure enough! The water was purified, just as Elisha had said.

— **2 Kings 2:1-22 (TLB)**
*HOLY BIBLE*

There is nothing that God hath established in a constant course of nature, and which therefore is done every day, but would seem a miracle, and exercise our admiration, if it were done but once.

**— John Donne**
*Oxford Dictionary of Quotations*

In 1953 George Clay was pastoring a small church in Galena, Kansas. But the church could not support his growing family so George took a job working at a funeral home, driving the hearse, which also did double duty as a community ambulance.

One morning in the middle of his shift, a call came that there had been an accident at a nearby electrical plant and two injured people needed immediate transport to a hospital in Baxter Springs, Kansas.

George climbed into the ambulance and raced to the electrical plant. His passengers loaded, he traced the route to Baxter Springs in his mind. The route over two-lane roads winding through the countryside at speeds sometimes exceeding 100 miles per hour was always treacherous. But at this time of day, he knew he would have to be especially alert for slow-moving farm equipment that might appear unexpectedly. There was also a narrow, one-lane bridge just before Baxter Springs that could pose a problem. Still, the approach on either side was fairly straight and he would not have to face oncoming traffic without warning.

He whispered a prayer for his passengers' needs and their safety, turned on the siren and lights, and sped away.

All went well for the first part of the trip. He was able to maintain "emergency speed" for the most part while keeping the ride as comfortable as possible for his injured passengers,

one of whom was able to sit up and watch out the front windshield. Ahead lay the long, one-laned bridge.

Suddenly, from a dirt road just before and right beside the bridge, a pickup truck entered the highway. It turned immediately onto the bridge, going in the same direction as the ambulance. A woman was driving and a small child stood on the seat beside her. The ambulance was going over 100 miles per hour and was only 50 to 75 feet from the pickup when it entered the road. There wasn't even time for George to brake.

"Lord, help me!" George cried aloud. What happened next took only a couple of seconds, but George says that even today he can see it as vividly as though it just happened. He saw two great hands slide down on either side of the ambulance—and then they were gone. George wasn't even sure that he was still alive when he looked back through his rear-view mirror to see what had happened to the truck. It was nowhere in sight. Only a few seconds had passed; it would have taken much longer for the truck to shift to reverse and somehow back out of the bridge. And yet a full view of the bridge behind him showed no trace of the vehicle.

The passenger sitting up also saw the truck and braced for impact. George still doesn't know if he also saw the hands; but they both witnessed the appearance, and then disappearance, of the pickup.

Could we see a miracle from God, how would our thoughts be affected with a holy awe and veneration of His presence! But if we consider everything as God's doing, either by order or permission, we shall then be affected with common things as they would be who saw a miracle. For as there is nothing to affect you in a miracle but as it is the action of God and bespeaks His presence, so when you consider God as acting in all things and all events, then all things will become venerable to you like miracles, and fill you with the same awful sentiments of the divine presence.

— **William Law**
*A Diary of Readings*
by John Baillie
Collier Books, 1986

# MIRACLES
## ARE HEAVEN SENT

irst grief swept over Janice. Her husband Edmond was obviously dead beside her in the airplane. Then panic threatened to overwhelm her as she realized that she alone was left to get the small aircraft back on the ground. Janice had never had a flying lesson.

Her attempts to raise someone with the radio backfired when she changed the settings so drastically that she could neither send nor receive any communication. She realized that whatever happened would be up to her and God. Trying to settle herself, Janice began to praise God. As she did, a strange calm came over her. Suddenly she realized that the plane was staying level all by itself due to special equipment, a leveler, that the plane they normally flew didn't have. Praise God for that!

Next, she surveyed the dials and switches to see if she recognized anything. Everything except the altimeter, speed indicator and compass were a mystery to her. Then she found a set of written directions she had never seen before. The instructions used only those instruments she understood and told her how to fly north.

Using the stick as she had seen her husband do, she was able to turn the plane. She realized she needed to be at a lower altitude, so she pushed forward on the stick.

Once again, because of the leveler, this worked and she began descending. For nearly two hours, she looked for an airstrip.

Eventually Janice picked out what looked like a clearing and headed toward it. At that moment the engine of the plane began to sputter and she saw that the gas gauge registered empty. The plane began dropping fast and touched down in a sparsely wooded area well short of her intended site. As she whizzed across the ground, the saplings in the newly reforested area began to slow the plane and it eventually came to rest on the edge of a dirt road adjoining her original target. It was then that Janice realized that there was nothing which would have slowed her forward motion at her intended site and she most likely would have run head-long into a dense, mature grove of trees.

Later, as the entire situation was analyzed, Janice realized that God spared her life with a series of miracles: the instructions, the leveler, and an empty gas tank, to name only three.

In September, Terry Shafer was strolling the shops in Moline, Illinois. She knew exactly what she wanted to get her husband, David, for Christmas, but she realized it might be too expensive. A little shop on Fifth attracted her attention, so she popped inside. Her eyes darted toward the corner display. "That's it!" she smiled as she nodded with pleasure. "How much?" she asked the shopkeeper.

"Only $127.50."

Her smile faded into disappointment as she realized David's salary couldn't stand such a jolt. He was feeding and clothing the family on a policeman's wage. It was out of the question. Yet she hated to give up without a try, so she applied a little persistence.

"Uh, what about putting this aside for me? Maybe I could pay a little each week, then pick it up a few days before Christmas?"

"No," the merchant said, "I won't do that." Then he smiled. "I'll gift-wrap it right now. You can take it with you and pay me later," he said. Terry was elated. She agreed to pay so much every week, then thanked and thanked the man as she left, explaining how delighted her husband would be.

"Oh, that's nothing at all," the shopkeeper answered, not realizing the significant role his generosity would play in the days ahead.

Then came Saturday, October 1. Patrolman David Shafer, working the night shift, got a call in his squad car. A drug store robbery was in progress. David reacted instantly, arriving on the scene just in time to see the suspect speed away. With siren screaming and lights flashing, he followed in hot pursuit. Three blocks later the getaway vehicle suddenly pulled over and stopped. The driver didn't move. David carefully approached the suspect with his weapon drawn. When he was only three feet from the driver's door, two things happened in a split second. The door flew open as the thief produced a .45-caliber pistol and fired at David's abdomen.

At seven o'clock that morning a patrolman came to the door of the Shafer home. Calmly and with great care, he told Terry what had happened.

Her husband had been pursuing a robbery suspect. There had been gunfire. David was hit. Shot at point-blank range.

Stunned, Terry thought how glad she was that she had not waited until Christmas to give her husband his present. How grateful she was that the shopkeeper had been willing to let her pay for it later. Otherwise, David would have surely died. Instead, he was now in the hospital—not with a gunshot wound, but with only a bad bruise.

You see, David was wearing the gift of life Terry could not wait to give—his brand-new bulletproof vest.

*The Finishing Touch*, Charles Swindoll, copyright © 1994, Word, Inc., Dallas, TX. All rights reserved.

When Frank heard God saying to him in his spirit, "Go preach My Gospel," he responded immediately. Since Frank had no education, he decided the first step he should take in preparing himself to preach would be to attend a good school. Only one thing stood in Frank's way — he had no money and no friends or family who might help support him. Still, he was determined to study and then preach.

Frank decided to attend a school that was five hundred miles away from his home. He had only five dollars in his pocket, so the only way he knew to get to the school was to walk. A friend asked him as he packed his bag and prepared to head out on foot, "How are you going to get there with no money?" Frank asked. "I have money. I have $5 and God's note."

The friend replied, "God's note? What's that?" Frank answered, "God's note in His Word that He will supply all my need according to His riches in glory by Christ Jesus."*

The friend asked, "Well, does that include dollars?"

Frank said, "I have to conclude that it means all my need." On the strength of that belief, Frank headed out.

Driver after driver stopped to offer Frank rides, until he

ultimately reached his destination without paying a cent. When he arrived at the school, he was offered a way to work while he studied. When others saw his diligence and his success in studying, they offered to help with financial gifts. On graduation day, Frank still had the same $5 bill in his pocket that he had started out with three years previously!

During his three years in school, Frank was never hungry. He always had a roof over his head and decent clothing to wear. He made many fine friends and succeeded greatly in his studies. In fact, Frank went on not only to preach but to be the president of a university!

He eventually framed the $5 bill he had carried for years in his pocket as a statement of his faith to the students who entered his office that God could supply all their needs, no matter how great they might be.

*See Philippians 4:19.*

Susie had been to the best physicians in her area. They had all diagnosed her with the same condition: heart disease in its final stages. They advised her to prepare herself to die. The woman had no reason to doubt their opinion. She was so weak she could only sit up for a little while at a time.

While lying in bed one day, Susie read a little book that included a commentary on a Bible verse that says, "What things soever ye desire, when ye pray, believe that ye receive them, and ye shall have them."* Susie laid down the book, slipped off the bed onto her knees, and told God that she desired to be well to enjoy her life with her husband and two children. She promised to put God first in her life and to make the best of whatever He gave to her. Susie felt no change in her body when she got back into bed. But that night she found she had strength to tuck her children into bed and to put a few things out for breakfast the next morning.

Susie slept well that night, but when she arose in the morning, her body was filled with pain from head to toe. Even so, she forced herself to get dressed. She reminded God that she was trusting in Him completely to provide for her, and that she desired to be of use to her family. She then went into the kitchen, and to the surprise of her husband, she prepared breakfast for her family and for five hired workers.

The young woman who had been helping the family with various housekeeping chores had resigned the day before Susie prayed. So when Susie's husband left for a full day of work, he encouraged her to return to bed and said he would try to find a girl to help.

Susie began to clear away the breakfast dishes, intending only to work as long as she had energy. But before she knew it, she had washed all of the dishes. She felt no great surge of strength, but she still had a little energy so she decided to prepare some clothes for washing. Little by little she worked, and by ten o'clock, she realized that she had only two more items to hand wash. So she finished washing them and prepared to take the large basket of clean, wet clothes she had accumulated outside to hang them on the clothesline. At that point, great pain and a "sinking feeling" hit her body. Susie felt as if she was staring death in the face. She dropped the full load of clothes, and although she was in intense agony, she stomped her foot on the ground and said, "I desire to be well and I believe that God is going to give me what I desire." No sooner had she spoken these words than the pain subsided and she picked up the basket and proceeded to hang the clothes on the line. When she threw the first sheet over the line, she felt as if something like a gauze netting began to part at the top of her head and fall down over her face and off the ends of her fingers all the way down past her toes. She stretched her arms their whole length toward the sky and straightened and stretched her body upward. As she did so, great health and strength filled her entire body! She knew without any doubt that she had been healed completely and a flood of joy filled her to overflowing.

Susie returned to her doctors a few days later. To their great amazement, they could find no trace of the heart disease that they had so carefully documented in previous months.

*See Mark 11:24*

Emily was the light of their lives. As a baby, she had a stroke, but her medical condition soon improved. In the next few years, her parents, although grateful for her recovery, still continued to watch her and to pray for her continuing good health.

One summer, the family decided to take a long road trip with Emily's grandparents. Everything proceeded according to schedule. The weather cooperated, the drive was pleasant, and everyone was healthy.

Except Emily. One morning, somewhere in Wyoming, she was more tired than usual. Then, she began vomiting. When attempts to make her feel better failed, her parents knew that they had to get her to a hospital immediately.

As the van approached a sizable town, Emily's parents had a new concern: How would they ever find the hospital? The situation called for some divine guidance.

Close to the town, the family scanned the road ahead. And there it was—on the shoulder: a hospital sign! A short distance from the first sign was a second, and later, a third and a fourth. The family was able to follow the signs straight to the building.

Emily, the doctor said, had had a mild epileptic seizure. She was treated and given a room for the night. Her mother realized then how scared she'd been, and how blessed Emily was to have received prompt medical attention.

"We might not have made it here if it hadn't been for the hospital signs on the road into town," Emily's mother told the doctor. "They were a lifesaver."

"What signs?" the doctor asked, puzzled. "There are no hospital signs on that road. I travel that road every day."

Emily's father and grandfather had taken the van to a gas station some miles away, and returned to the hospital—late.

"We were on the same road as before," they said. "We thought we could follow the signs back to the hospital, but they weren't there."

The next day, a call to the local Chamber of Commerce confirmed the signs' nonexistence. (Signs have since been put up.)

This experience gave Emily's family a new meaning for the prayer, "God, give me a sign."

In the same sense that everything may be said to be a mystery, so also may it be said that everything is a miracle, and that no one thing is a greater miracle than another. The elephant, though larger, is not a greater miracle than a mite; nor a mountain a greater miracle than an atom. To an almighty power it is no more difficult to make the one than the other, and no more difficult to make a million worlds than to make one.

— **Thomas Paine**

Rain was pouring as Jill climbed the steps from the subway station and walked out onto the busy streets of London. A quick survey of the intersection before her confirmed her fear: no taxis in sight and literally dozens of people eagerly waiting to hail one.

She picked up her two suitcases and began to walk in the general direction of her hotel, which she knew to be at least ten blocks away. Within seconds she was drenched, but the rain was not her greatest concern. She had heard that this particular neighborhood next to the subway station was not among the safest in the city, and evening darkness was falling fast. She quickened her step, although that was difficult to do given the weight of her luggage.

When she was halfway down the first long, narrow block, she suddenly heard the beep of a horn. She turned, startled to see a taxi driver peering at her through a half-opened window. "Need a lift, missy?" he asked with cheer in his voice.

"Oh, yes! Thank you!" she exclaimed, amazed at his presence. As he hurried from the taxi to take her bags and toss them into the trunk of his car, she quickly glanced back toward the subway station. Groups of people

remained clustered at each corner of the intersection, still eagerly lifting their hands in an attempt to wave down each passing taxi, all of which had passengers. She slid into the back seat of the taxi before her, gave the driver the name of her hotel, and the car sped quickly down the street. Scores of people were standing at each intersection they passed, many of whom attempted at least a partial wave at her cab as it passed by.

Within a few minutes the cab arrived at Jill's hotel. She noticed as the driver took her bags from the car that he was dressed in a white shirt and white jeans. How odd, Jill thought, to be wearing white on a muddy, rainy day like this? I've never seen a cab driver dressed like this in London.

The cab driver accepted her payment and generous tip with a hearty smile, and then climbed back into his taxi and sped away.

As Jill waited to register for her room at the hotel, she thought it strange that he didn't take any passengers with him. Could this cab driver that seemed to have come from thin air possibly have been...?

Of one thing she was certain. He had given her a miracle moment.

For all the tired and needy,
For all the rich and proud,
For all the sick and weary,
For all the bent and bowed,
There's one electric moment
The instant you believe,
Just touch His hand of healing,
By faith you will receive.

The God of miracles is reaching out His hand,
The God of miracles is moving through the
        land.
So touch Him, believe Him, this moment as
        you pray.
Now expect a miracle, and a miracle is yours
        today.

— **Ralph Carmichael**

*The God of Miracles* by Ralph Carmichael, Adm. by EMI
Christian Music Publishing.  Used by permission.

God works through human beings. How much more effective He can be when we offer Him our lives and our faith in the absolute belief that He can accomplish anything. We become witnesses to His power and love.

God's answer to an individual's prayer—and God always answers—is a private matter between the person and God. Even though the person may tell others of God's works on his behalf, not everyone will believe. After all, it's just one person's word. But five persons? Ten? Hundreds? Who can dispute the power of God when so many of us can witness to His miracles?

— **Phyllis Hobe**
*The Guideposts Handbook of Prayer*
Guideposts Associates, Inc.
1982

If you visit the Chapel of Our Lady of Light in Santa Fe, New Mexico, you will see a miracle of both legendary and factual dimensions. The legendary part relates mostly to how the miracle came to be; but, in fact, the miracle continues to exist today and no one has been able to explain it.

Here's the story: In the late nineteenth century, the bishop responsible for a convent school in Santa Fe commissioned a French architect named Projectus Mouly of Paris to design a chapel for the school and to pattern it after the Sainte Chapelle in Paris. Mouly designed a beautiful structure with a balcony choir loft set in front of the magnificent stained-glass window that rested under the front eave of the church. But the absent-minded architect forgot to include a staircase to reach the loft and, alas, the structure was completed without access to the choir loft except by ladder. Furthermore, there seemed to be no place to install a staircase.

Master carpenter after master carpenter visited the chapel in hopes of coming up with a solution; but all went away without success. When hope was all but lost, an unusual-looking stranger appeared and began work, even though he didn't have any particular agreement with the

Mother Superior in charge. Day after day he arrived at the chapel with loads of lumber, working until at last he came no more. The sisters crept into the chapel to view the finished product and couldn't believe their eyes.

Today, the wonder stands as it first did more than 100 years ago when the chapel was dedicated. A double-spiral staircase made entirely of a hard wood not found anywhere in New Mexico spirals from the floor of the chapel to the loft above with no visible means of support. The staircase has thirty-three steps—one for each year of Christ's life on earth. They ascend in perfect symmetry from a small space in the corner through the air to the loft above. The staircase is as solid a structure as it would be if supported every few feet by undergirding. Architects scratch their heads and tourists gawk.

There are no nails in the structure, only wooden pegs. The curved stringers are put together with absolute precision. The wood is spliced in seven places on the inside and nine on the outside. School records show that no payment for the staircase was ever made.

Legend has it that the staircase was made by a man known only as Jose (Joseph)—and that he was a carpenter.

Six Soviet cosmonauts said they witnessed the most awe-inspiring spectacle ever encountered in space—a band of glowing angels with wings as big as jumbo jets. Cosmonauts Vladimir Solovev, Oleg Atkov, and Leonid Kizim said they first saw the celestial beings during their 155th day aboard the orbiting Salyat 7 space station.

"What we saw," they said, "were seven giant figures in the shape of humans, but with wings and mistlike halos, as in the classic depiction of angels. Their faces were round with cherubic smiles." Twelve days later the figures returned and were seen by three other Soviet scientists, including woman cosmonaut Svetlana Asvitskaya. "They were smiling," she said, "as though they shared a glorious secret."

Some years ago, Dr. S. W. Mitchell, a well-known neurologist in Philadelphia concluded that he must have seen an angel. It was the only explanation that made sense to him. After a very tiring day he had turned in early. But he was awakened by a persistent knocking at his door. He opened the door to find a little girl, poorly dressed and deeply upset. She explained briefly that her mother was very sick and needed his help. Even though it was a bitterly cold and snowy night and Dr. Mitchell was bone-weary, he dressed and followed the little girl.

He found her mother desperately ill with pneumonia. After treating her, the doctor complimented the sick woman on her daughter's courage and persistence in coming to get him. The woman gave him a strange look and said, "Doctor, my daughter died a month ago. Her shoes and coat are in the closet there." Dr. Mitchell went to the closet and opened the door. There hung the very coat that he had seen on the little girl. It was warm and dark, however, and could not possibly have just been hung up after a walk on a snowy night.

The angels are white flaming white and the eye that would confront them shrivels

and there's no other way you've got to become like stone if you want their company

and when you look for the miracle you've got to scatter your blood to the eight points of the wind

because the miracle is nowhere but circulating in the veins of man.

— **George Seferis**
*"Les Anges Sont Blancs"*

# MIRACLES
## ARE HEAVEN SENT

A sweet rosy-cheeked baby was born to German parents in northern Italy. The picture of health at its birth, the baby was vaccinated against smallpox when it was only three days old. The vaccination was repeated again at eight days since the baby's mother had been exposed to smallpox. But those attending the child and its mother feared the worst.

Almost immediately after the second vaccination, the baby began to wither. Her round face and body became a skeleton of skin and bones as her baby features turned into those of an old woman's wrinkled face. She had no spasms or convulsions, but she was fading away day by day. Nothing the physician or others did seemed to make any difference. When she was four weeks old, the day seemed to have come when the baby's last feeble breath would pass her lips.

The physician who was attending the mother and baby came to the side of the cradle and whispered to the woman who was watching over the baby, "I will stay with you. It will be over in two or three minutes." The baby had already taken on the look of a corpse.

The woman at the baby's side, however, felt a leaping in her heart. She cried out, "Lord, I cannot let her go!" Then before the physician could stop her, she took the baby out of the cradle, carried her into her bedroom, laid the baby on her own bed and fell on her knees. She cried, "Lord, take all that I have, but leave this child to her mother!"

The Bible story of Elijah and the Zarephath widow's son* flashed through her mind. So she leaned over the child, put her face on the baby's face, opened the baby's lips, and breathed three times into her little mouth. Instantly, the "old woman's features" disappeared as the little face before her began to turn the sweetest pink blush. The baby opened her eyes and smiled. Anxious to show the baby to the doctor, the woman quickly scooped up the infant and went back into the room where he was waiting. Expecting the woman to return and hand him a corpse, he nearly collapsed to the floor when he found that she had handed him a rosy-faced baby. "What have you done to the child?" he gasped. "Nothing," the woman answered. "God did it all."

*See I Kings 17:17-23

## MIRACLES
### ARE HEAVEN SENT

"The God we serve is a God Who knows no limit!"

God is unlimited . . . yet man limits an unlimited God.

God is completely unlimited as to time or space or condition . . . or to any concept for that matter. He is all powerful, all authoritative, all creative.

Absolutely nothing is impossible to Him.

There is no limit to His ability, no limit to His love, no limit to His mercy, no limit to His bountifulness, no limit to His desire to bless His people.

He is completely unlimited . . . yet most people, even Christians, limit an unlimited God. They see Him in such narrow concepts.

Man is a creature so infinitely inferior to the Creator God that it is hard to imagine how man can have any power with God. Yet he does.

Made of the dust of the earth, enjoying life only by the inbreathing of God, absolutely dependent on God for all provision . . . yet man has both the power and the proneness to limit God to the tiniest fraction of what God would and could be in that life and in that experience.

There are many, many ways and reasons why we limit an unlimited God.

Many of these reasons have to do with background or environment. Many of them have to do with tradition. God has been presented to us within certain limits by our parents, our pastors, our teachers, our peers . . . and we see Him only within those limits.

"That's the way it is" or "That's the way we do it" gets to be the program and the practice in our churches and in our lives.

"That's the way it has always been done."

"That's the way my grandmother did it."

"That's the tradition."

We also limit God by our experiences or our natural ability to experience.

How often people say, "Show me a miracle, and I will believe, but until then, I won't believe anything I don't see. I won't accept anything I can't touch."

There is a main reason that we limit an unlimited God. It is at the base, the root of all the other reasons we might give.

It is this: We limit an unlimited God because we do not see Him as He really is.

**— Morris Cerullo**

*How to Take the Limit Off of God,* by Morris Cerullo, World Evangelism, San Diego, CA 92123. Used by permission.

Soon after she came to the orphanage in Jugdalpur, India, Keurin became known as "the doctor." A severe and frequently fatal eye disease raged among the children that year. Many of the youngsters died in great pain in spite of every effort of the physicians. Keurin served night and day with great devotion, nursing and helping to comfort those who were suffering.

After several months, the scourge seemed to pass, leaving a number of the surviving children blind in one or both eyes. Yet Keurin's eyes remained healthy throughout the plague.

A month after the last child had been restored to health, Keurin fell ill. The disease had taken hold in her eyes. Although the children and the missionaries in charge of the orphanage prayed earnestly, Keurin lost her sight over a period of two weeks. Those around her tried to comfort her with the hope that God must have something better in store for her than her eyesight. But Keurin would hear none of their encouraging words. At least a dozen times a day, the orphanage personnel found her praying aloud in her room for the return of her eyesight.

The next year, a visiting minister held a midday service at the orphanage at which he prayed for the children who were sick. As he was preparing to leave, a growing cry began to surge through the orphanage, "Keurin is coming." Thinking that Keurin was making her way to the minister for prayer, the orphanage director quickly moved to help her navigate the way across the crowded plaza where they were standing. Keurin, however, needed no assistance. As she came toward the minister, her pace quickened. Then she took the hand of the orphanage director and exclaimed, "God has opened my eyes!" Keurin could see again. After nearly a year of blindness, her eyesight had returned within a matter of minutes! Even though others had lost hope for a miracle, Keurin had not!

Miracles do happen. They are an almost daily occurrence, and I am persuaded that they can happen to all who are willing to open themselves up to this very real probability.

It doesn't seem that there are any rules to follow or requirements that must be met before a miracle can take place, but it does appear that these marvelous and miraculous phenomena happen most often to those who are willing to reach out and seek such help in a spirit of love and service.

— **Charles E. Sellier**

In 1977, unusually cold weather conditions threatened to destroy Norvel Hayes' orange groves in Florida. The trees in the area were covered with icicles, and the orange growers knew from past experience that it was highly likely that the cold would kill their crops and possibly the trees themselves.

But Norvel wasn't willing to accept the disaster that seemed inevitable. He believed God could save his trees, and he asked for a miracle.

"I got in my car, drove to the orange grove and parked along the highway," he said. "I looked at the grove and told the devil to take his hands off the orange trees. Then I asked the Father, in Jesus' name, to let His power come and hover around my fruit trees and not let them die."

A few days later the sun began to shine and things warmed up. Norvel still gets excited when he describes the results of his prayer. "Fruit was developing on my trees! The twenty-five hundred orange trees on the property across the road, which was owned by another grower, were dead.

But on my side of the road, it was different. It was as though a shield had been placed on my property line, which stopped the potentially damaging frost from crossing it. I didn't lose a tree."

$\mathbf{M}$issionary Morris Plotts tells an extraordinary story that occurred during the Mau Mau uprisings in East Africa in 1956. A band of roving Mau Maus massacred the entire village of Lauri—including women and children—and headed for Rift Valley Academy, a Christian school less than three miles away, where the children of missionaries in the field were being boarded and educated. The Mau Maus were armed with torches, spears, bows and arrows, and clubs, determined to destroy the school. Before they arrived, however, a fast-running messenger brought news of the massacre to the academy. The children were terrified upon hearing what had happened at Lauri, but there was nowhere to flee. Their only resource was prayer.

In the night, the teachers and children saw torches approaching the school and soon a ring of the torches surrounded the structure, cutting off any avenue of escape. Angry curses could be heard coming from the warriors as the circle closed tighter and tighter. Finally, the warriors drew close enough to begin throwing their spears, but instead, they suddenly stopped, then began to retreat and finally fled into the jungle.

A rescuing Army that had been sent in response to an emergency call arrived shortly afterward, but the Mau Maus were nowhere to be found. The army spread out in search of them and eventually captured the entire band. Before a judge, the leader of the Mau Maus admitted the massacre at Lauri and their intent to attack the school at Rift Valley. "Why didn't you?" asked the judge.

"We were on our way to attack and destroy all the people at the school. But as we came closer, all of a sudden between us and the school, there were many huge men, dressed in white with flaming swords. We became afraid and we ran to hide."

One evening as Emperor Alexander of Russia was making his way across Bavaria, he shut himself up in a hotel room and exclaimed aloud, "Oh, that some holy soul might be sent to me who could solve the great enigma of my life and destiny!" He was emotionally and physically exhausted.

At that very moment, Prince Wollonsky opened the door to the room and announced that Madame Krudener was waiting outside his room insisting to see him. The Emperor replied, "Surely she comes in answer to my prayer; let her enter."

Baroness Von Krudener had met the Emperor previously and had won his confidence with her spirit of prophecy. She had a fearless love of truth, and a simple piety. For three hours, she counseled the monarch, who later said, "She spoke music to my spirit and brought me a peace that no other on earth could give."

Before she left, Madame Krudener said she had come to plead the cause of the starving peasants in Russia. The Emperor responded by exhausting his royal coffers to send provisions to those who were suffering.

But that wasn't all that resulted from her miraculously timed visit with the Emperor. In the years that followed,

Madame Krudener held religious meetings three times a week which were attended by the princes, nobles, and great generals of Europe. She preached and taught them God's plan for the human soul. This was something no other human being at that time was bold enough or in a privileged enough position to do. God had given her entree not only to help Alexander and the starving peasants in Russia, but to preach His Word to the power structure of an entire continent.

The British express train raced through the night, its powerful headlamp spearing the black darkness ahead. The train was carrying Queen Victoria.

Suddenly the engineer saw a startling sight. Revealed in the beam of the engine's headlights was a weird figure in a black cloak standing in the middle of the tracks and waving its arms. The engineer grabbed for the brakes and brought the train to a grinding halt.

He and his fellow trainsmen climbed out to see what had stopped them. They could find no trace of the strange figure. On a hunch, the engineer walked a few yards farther up the tracks. Suddenly he stopped and stared into the fog in horror. A bridge had been washed out and had fallen into a swollen stream. If he had not heeded the ghostly figure, the train would have plunged into the stream.

While the bridge and tracks were being repaired, the crew made a more intensive search for the strange flagman. But not until they got to London did they solve the mystery. At the base of the engine's headlamp was a huge moth. The engineer looked at it for a moment, then on impulse wet its wings and pasted it to the glass of the lamp. Climbing back into his cab, he switched on the lamp and saw the "phantom flagman" in the beam. He quickly realized what had happened: the moth had flown into the beam seconds before the train had reached the washed-out bridge. In the fog, it appeared to be a phantom figure waving its arms.

When Queen Victoria was told of the strange happening, she said, "I'm sure it was no accident. It was God's way of protecting us."

They had prayed for her at the breakfast table when the whole family was together, but now Mattie had the impulse to put her hand through the open car window and pray for her daughter one more time before Annie drove away. This time she prayed specifically that God would send His angels to protect Annie as she drove the eleven hours back to college for her senior year, and to bring her back home safely.

"Aw, Mom, I'm gonna be fine!" But Annie knew she could use all the prayers her mom was praying. She had traveled alone before, but never for this long nor as the sole driver of a car.

Annie was about three hours from home—not quite to the state line—when it happened. A semi-trailer truck jackknifed in front of her and she steered to the side to avoid a head-on collision. Suddenly Annie's little car was rolling over and over and over down a steep embankment.

Cars stopped and people rushed down the embankment to try to free Annie. Imagine their amazement to see Annie standing beside the severely crushed overturned car! "Can you help me set it up and push it up the hill?" she said.

"Darlin'," a trucker replied, "how did you get out of there? You'd better lie down!"

"I'm fine," Annie insisted.

Hours later, back at home, Annie recalled how only minutes before the crash, she felt clearly impressed to try and find the seat belts in the old model Volkswagen. She had never worn them before and she didn't even know if the car had any. (This was several years before seat-belt awareness campaigns and state laws made seat-belt use the norm.) She finally dug them out from under the seat and snapped the ends together. It was an act that probably saved her life.

A second miracle joined the first. A Christian family traveling in the opposite direction saw the crash and, after determining Annie didn't need immediate medical care, they insisted on turning around and driving Annie all the way back home before continuing on their trip.

God had answered Mattie's prayer in full.

wo ministers were called to Alma's hospital room while she was dying. She had already slipped into a coma and the nurse on duty bluntly told the ministers as they arrived at her bedside that they were too late. Alma could no longer speak, hear, or see, and there was no hope of her recovery.

The ministers proceeded as if they hadn't heard the nurse. They knelt by Alma's bedside, shared with her God's plan for the salvation of her soul and their belief that she would recover. Then the two men prayed for both her soul and body. They detected no movement and saw no response from her, yet both men had no doubt that Alma had heard them "in her spirit."

Weeks passed and the two ministers heard no further word about Alma. They both became so busy in the normal course of their ministry that they had all but forgotten their visit to her bedside. Then . . . one afternoon Alma's mother-in-law came to their church to tell them how God had healed Alma! Several weeks later, Alma herself came into their office and said, "As you knelt by my bedside, I became aware that someone was there. The sound of your voices was different than the other voices I had been hearing. As you prayed for me, it was as if the words were actually coming into my body. I felt my soul growing quiet. I heard a voice tell me how to have faith in God, and somehow, in a way I can't quite describe, I felt faith stirring inside me. I couldn't speak to tell you, but at that moment, I knew that I was going to get well and that I would one day go home from the hospital."

The two ministers rejoiced with Alma, then one of them said, "I just have one question for you." One of the men responded, "What is it?"

"Who told you that I was in the hospital? I've never been to your church and I don't know anybody in this city except my mother-in-law."

The ministers glanced at each other, then one of them confessed, "Our secretary gave us a message that read, 'Urgent that you pray. Hospital room 537.' That was the room you were in, Alma. As we were leaving the hospital, we checked the patient roster and discovered that one of our parishioners was in room 357. Our secretary had inverted the numbers, but God knew who really needed our prayers that day."

In the early 1900s, when physicians advised Victoria to spend some time in southern California for her "health's sake," she and her husband followed their advice and moved to Los Angeles, California. At the time, Victoria was paralyzed in both knees and hadn't been able to walk for three years. Her spine was diseased, and her eyesight had greatly failed.

After Victoria had been in California for a year, she heard about a woman who was praying for the sick in a tent at Sixtieth and Pasadena Streets. She and her husband attended the meeting and after Victoria received prayer, she found that her eyesight was instantly restored. All pain had also left her body. In an exuberant act of joy, she sat on her glasses and broke them in pieces, announcing to all around her that she felt "just like a new-born baby."

Victoria's husband, who had massaged his wife's body with alcohol and liniments for three years, had never trusted God for his own healing from kidney and stomach ailments. As a Jew, he believed in God, but was unsure about the possibility of having a personal relationship with the Almighty. When he saw the immediate change in his wife, he said, "I am going to ask the Lord to heal me, too." The next day, he also was healed.

Four months later he wrote to his parents in Germany about all that had happened to him spiritually and physically, and they asked their son to send them a New Testament in German so they might know more. In the reading of the Christian Scriptures, they became convinced of their need for a personal Savior. Impressed with the healing miracle stories of Jesus, the parents gave the New Testament to their sick daughter, and she was healed as she read the gospels!

One miracle very often triggers others!

When we observe the needle of the mariner, without visible organ, or sense of faculty, pointing with a trembling and pious fidelity to the unseen pole, and guiding, no one favored people only, but all nations, at all times, across a wilderness of waters, so that a ship sails forth from one shore and strikes the narrowest inlet or bay on the other side of the globe, why ought we not to be filled with awe as reverential and as religious as though we had seen the pillar of cloud by day, and of fire by night, which led the children of Israel in their journey through the wilderness?

**— Horace Mann**
*The Christian Reader*
*Stanley Irving Steiber, Editor*
*Association Press, 1952*

# Conclusion

The presence of the Miracle Worker, the Lord Jesus Christ, and His miraculous works are around us continually. They increase our understanding of *God's inability to fail us* in any area of life; they encourage us to be *obedient to the Spirit of God*, for thereby we will, at times, be a part of someone else's miracle — carrying God's mercy, grace, love, compassion, healing, delivering and resurrection power to them; and they make us more sensitive to His presence and to His willingness to help us.

As you continue to enjoy the true accounts in *Miracles Are Heaven Sent*, may you be motivated and energized by the Spirit of the living God to **press toward the mark for the prize of the high calling of God in Christ Jesus** as never before (Philippians 3:14), knowing He is both able and willing to give you wisdom and provision for whatever is needed to complete your destiny. In fact, He is willing to do **exceeding abundantly above all that we ask or think, according to the power that worketh in us** (Ephesians 3:20).

Even the world (the Pharisees) said of Jesus, **Here is this man performing many miraculous signs** (John 11:47 NIV). First John 3:2 NKJV says **we shall be like Him.** May your walk in Christ be enriched as you personally experience the miracles that are Heaven sent!